25

THE GOD
OF
SECOND
CHANCES

EXPERIENCING HIS GRACE FOR
THE BEST OF YOUR LIFE

STEPHEN ARTERBURN

THOMAS NELSON
Since 1798

NASHVILLE   DALLAS   MEXICO CITY   RIO DE JANEIRO

My thanks to Larry Sonnenburg,
Sharon Barnes, Kim Dixon, and
Cheryl Lampe, who encouraged me to give
this little book a second chance.

Published in Nashville, Tennessee, by Thomas Nelson. Thomas Nelson is a registered trademark of Thomas Nelson, Inc.

Published in association with the literary agency of Alive Communications, Inc. 7680 Goddard Street, Suite 200, Colorado Springs, CO 80920. www.alivecommunications.com

Thomas Nelson, Inc., titles may be purchased in bulk for educational, business, fund-raising, or sales promotional use. For information, please e-mail SpecialMarkets@ThomasNelson.com.

Unless otherwise noted, Scripture quotations are taken from the Holy Bible, New International Version®, NIV®. ©1973, 1978, 1984 by Biblica, Inc. Used by permission of Zondervan. All rights reserved worldwide.

The Scripture quotation noted from *The Message* is taken from *The Message* by Eugene H. Peterson. © 1993, 1994, 1995, 1996, 2000. Used by permission of NavPress Publishing Group. All rights reserved.

Previously published as a portion of *Surprised by God*, a Focus on the Family book, Tyndale House Publishers, 1997. Also previously published as a portion of *The God of Second Chances*, a Focus on the Family book, Tyndale House Publishers, 1999.

ISBN 978-0-8499-4620-2 (trade paper)

Library of Congress Cataloging-in-Publication Data is available.

ISBN 978-0-7852-6569-6

Printed in the United States of America
10 11 12 13 14 RRD 5 4 3 2 1

CONTENTS

PART ONE

A SOUL DAMAGED

ONE

THE JOURNEY OF LIFE

Two Paths to Choose From

T hey called it the golden egg. I called it the Big One. It was Easter, and I was a three-year-old on an egg hunt. This was serious business. Candy, you must understand, was an extremely important part of my life. A lot of children had come with the same intent I had—to gather up as much candy and as many eggs as possible. I couldn't count at that time, but I remember thinking, *There must be a hundred kids here.*

Because I was so young, my mom let me watch the organizers hide the colored eggs and chocolates on the green rolling field where the hunt would take place. Before long, I had spotted the man with the Big One—a jumbo-sized, cream-filled chocolate egg wrapped in gold foil. He was off to the side of the field, jamming the prize egg into a hole where a water faucet pipe came up through the ground. I might have been only three, but I wasn't a fool. I knew an inside tip when I saw one. Call it a competitive edge in the bunny-eat-bunny world of Easter egg hunts.

All the kids were herded behind the starting line. Most of the others were much older and bigger than I was—but not wiser. With the word *Go!* the hunt started, and I made a bee-line for the Big One. It didn't matter how many colored eggs or chocolates lay in my path; I didn't stop to pick up the lesser, almost meaningless morsels. My legs, being puny three-year-old models, couldn't take me there fast enough. Relatively soon, however, I reached my destination. I glanced around. I was alone. The egg was mine, all mine.

But as I reached my hand into the shallow hole, my peewee face formed an expression you see only in old Hitchcock movies.

Huh? There's nothing here. The hole is empty.

Furiously my little hand searched again and again for what I knew was to be mine. It was not there. I couldn't believe it. I put my basket down and tried the other hand, as if the egg were there but I had lost the ability to feel with my right hand. My left hand also seemed to be numb since I again came up empty. I lay down on the grass and peered into the six-inch hole. I wasn't going to move until I found it. I started digging and pulling grass around that hole, but nothing I did uncovered the golden egg I had seen placed there.

At age three I wasn't able to consider the possibility that the man had moved the egg after I turned and walked back toward the starting line. I continued to search frantically while precious minutes slipped away and the other kids gathered up handfuls of goodies.

A loud scream from across the field broke my concentration. In an old oak tree, between two branches that hung low enough for kids to reach, a child had found the Big One. Lesley Waters. I still remember her name. As I ran across the field in disbelief, fake green grass flew from my otherwise empty basket. Looking around, I saw that all the other children's baskets were full to overflowing. When I spotted Lesley with the Big One, I started to cry. My mom came and made my brothers give me some of their candy. Talk about adding insult to injury—now I had a small pile of hand-me-down candy.

From the certainty of a sweet and calculated victory came the bitter taste of defeat. Still, the day wasn't a total loss, for I learned a valuable lesson: what promises to bring happiness and fulfillment often leaves us empty. Unfortunately it was a lesson I've had to learn again and again.

Most of us spend considerable time and energy searching for the Big One—whatever it is we think will bring lasting joy and satisfaction. We dream about it, sweat over it; even do without other, smaller things in its pursuit. For we know once we have achieved, possessed, owned, romanced, or conquered the Big One, our lives, once and for all, will be happy and fulfilling. This is true of most humans, not just three-year-olds on Easter egg hunts.

We desperately do not want to live our lives unloved, unknown, and feeling unalive. We search for meaning, pleasure, esteem, recognition, and freedom. These are not bad goals. The problem is how we try to achieve these goals, what path we take to attain them. We see the Big One, and we're sure it will bring us happiness. It might be in a pile of money, in the heart of a future spouse, on a nameplate on a desk, on the eighteenth green of a posh golf course—or, for that matter, anything that represents success in terms the world understands.

Proverbs 14:12 addresses our quest for fulfillment: "There is a way that seems right to a man, but in the end it leads to death." Often this death means not a literal trip to the grave but a spiritual death, which includes perpetual longing, emptiness, and futility. It is the feeling of a three-year-old in a giant green field, holding an empty basket with fake green grass stuck between two of your six teeth. The pursuit of the Big One has been not only a waste of time but also an utter embarrassment. You end up hating Lesley Waters, even though you would rather not. You just can't stand the way she dances around the oak tree.

The "way that seems right to a man" might be called the broad path. It is full of all the pleasures of this world. Here, you find money, sex, and power, which promise happiness but deliver deep emptiness. What seems so certain to fulfill you turns out to be an illusion. In the end the price you pay is your soul.

God desires more for our lives. He wants us to travel the narrow path, which brings fulfillment and meaning. The Bible tells us that those who follow this road must be committed to self-sacrifice, delayed gratification, responsibility, and integrity.

Part of the problem facing Christians is embracing the promises of God. We too often mistakenly think of Him as the Great Killjoy, performing acts of magic, complete with thunder and fanfare, to keep us miserably on our knees. Actually, though, Jesus said that a life committed to following Him will bring joy, freedom, intimacy, and genuine satisfaction. He said, "I have come that they may have life, and have it to the full," and "If you obey my commands, you will remain in my love . . . I have told you this so that my joy may be in you and that your joy may be complete" (John 10:10; 15:10–11).

But the fulfillment of these promises comes by walking a path we would never expect. The path to joy is a narrow one, and God continues to surprise us along the way. As Jesus said, "Enter through the narrow gate. For wide is the gate and broad is the road that leads to destruction, and many enter through it. But small is the gate and narrow the road that leads to life, and only a few find it" (Matt. 7:13–14).

With so much hope available to all of us who struggle, it is sad that we often find ourselves in seemingly hopeless situations. We're bombarded with endless pitches for the *something* that's "guaranteed" to bring happiness, and we can no longer hear the still, small voice of God leading us. We're promised quick fixes and instant solutions. Buy this car. Try this pill. Chant this mantra. Use this diet. Pursue this relationship.

It's incredible how many people tell us how to live and profess to have the inside track on the truth. And the majority of these people and their intricate systems of knowledge reject the truth of God.

There is one great truth and one great lie. The great truth is that God loves us, and through Him we find ultimate meaning and fulfillment. The great lie is that we can control our own destinies and find contentment on our own. When we leave the truth—the narrow and grace-filled path of God's love—we pursue the lie, the broad and deadly path, the lovely mirage of self-determination. The lie prompts us to try to "make life happen" by our own devices and schemes.

Unfortunately no matter how closely we follow God, no one is immune to straying. Even though we know better, we take the broad path once again, partly because the narrow path seems so demanding. Nevertheless, to find true joy and meaning in life, we must return to the truth and base our lives on the one source of guidance that never fails—God's Word, the Bible.

Those of us who call ourselves Christians know that the broad path steers us away from the one true God of the universe and toward the false gods of this world. These gods lead us to artificial joys, like mirages in the desert that deceive us with promises to quench our thirst. We know better. We have been warned thousands of times. Yet so often, we veer off course. Why? Because there is some satisfaction even in what is fake. Our needs feel met temporarily. It is no wonder we have a hard time staying on the narrow path to fulfillment and freedom. The world with its fake truth and counterfeit promises seems so appealing, so real, so accessible. Yet, as I noted earlier, Proverbs tells us that this path *always*—not *maybe* or *sometimes*—ends in death and destruction. Settling for the mediocre existence of a counterfeit life cuts us off from the surprising grace of God.

We all know people who look so good, so together. In our jealousy we want what they have. But we don't know that their happiness is shallow. We follow our perceptions of them instead of God's reality. We pursue the image that someone presents of the "good life," crafting our idols. In the end, however, we find out the person is morally bankrupt and the path has led us to destruction.

I once heard a story of a farmer who decided to sell his sheep at market. On the way there his truck caught on fire. He stopped immediately, lowered the truck's ramp, and led his sheep to safety. As he and the little flock stood near the burning vehicle, one of the sheep broke from the group and walked back up the ramp and into the fire. The rest of the sheep followed this "leader" to their deaths.

With our propensity to follow others who lead us astray, is it any wonder the Bible says we are like sheep?

In the journey of life, it matters tremendously which path

we choose. Many people pursue the gods of this age—money, power, possessions, control, comfort, pleasure—and worship at their altars, whatever the cost. They seek to find freedom in these gods but end up trapped. There has never been an age that 2 Peter 2:19 described more accurately: "They promise them freedom, while they themselves are slaves of depravity—for a man is a slave to whatever has mastered him." Our society, while claiming to be enlightened and progressive, is shackled with addiction, moral decay, violence, despair, and apathy. The age of self-fulfillment has led to self-destruction.

Despite the pain the broad road brings, too few of us spend enough time walking the narrow path, where real joy is available. By following Jesus we can know the truth and have it set us free. But living by freedom and grace is not easy because it takes discipline. It requires us to have faith in Jesus and give our lives to Him.

No one likes to give up control. We would rather buy the lies of the world than follow in the freedom of truth. Some of us buy the lie of *fate:* we are simply born a certain way, and our genes keep us from following the narrow path. Others buy the lie of *religion:* we would rather hold on to rules, hiding behind rituals and lists of dos and don'ts, than be in a loving relationship with an awesome God. Still others buy the lie of *having it all:* we want temporary satisfaction rather than eternal fulfillment. We often split ourselves in two by trying to straddle both paths. We end up confused and torn, never satisfied with what we have and never experiencing what we truly need.

Even for the most sincere Christians, life is filled with struggle, doubt, and frustration. If you don't struggle, if your faith has freed you from all worry and anxiety, you don't need this book. If you have become a Christian and everything has worked out perfectly for you, then I have nothing to offer. If you are completely immune from sexual temptation, or if your attitude toward money and material possessions has never been a problem, don't bother reading on. This book is for fellow strugglers who, even as they limp, want to move toward joy.

Most men and women reach a point where they decide to stop settling for mediocre lives. With growing disdain and regret, they search for something better, richer, deeper. Many people will give up everything to find authentic joy, a life full of purpose and integrity.

You may be there. You may be ready to let go of what is known and take a journey into the unknown—a journey full of fears, thrills, servanthood, and gratitude. You may be ready to give up the second best and seek the heights and depths of an unburdened relationship with God through Jesus Christ. You may be ready for life, real life.

Some misguided leaders tell us that following Christ brings one joyous experience after another. But following after God, the *real* One, often involves suffering, surrender, and patience. There are plenty of reasons that the path Jesus described is called *narrow*. In seeking after purpose and fulfillment, we often feel restrained by such pesky realities as *conscience* and *morality*. Because we follow God, we give up control of ourselves and often feel totally out of control.

But then the truth strikes us. We are surprised to discover that while it is not a pain-free existence, following God leads to real joy. By relinquishing self-control and giving ourselves away in the love of God, we experience deep and sustaining satisfaction. It is the path that, by the power and grace of God, can move us *through* pain to peace. It is the path that, by following after what is real and eternal, can bypass the false gods of this world, which ultimately bring only emptiness. It is the path that, through obedience, sets us free.

It is the path seldom followed, however. I should know. I am a prodigal son from a family of prodigal sons. My parents, who lived in deep faith, had three sons leave the narrow path to pursue their own ways. My dad made the biblical father of the prodigal son look like a rookie. My brothers and I had to find out for ourselves that the broad path, which looks so good, is a pain-filled lie. Even though each of us eventually came back, we did not escape the consequences of our sin.

This book is, in part, my life story. It tells how I left the narrow path as outlined in the Bible to pursue the false gods of our age and how my "successes" became bitter failures. In Part 1, I describe the pursuits that led me (and lead many others) off the narrow path and away from the joy that comes from following God. In Part 2, I discuss the flip side of those

empty pursuits—the choices and endeavors that bring ultimate healing, wholeness, and fulfillment.

By chasing after self-interests, I became spiritually and
emotionally bankrupt. Shocked by the consequences of self-
obsessive sin, I became suicidal. By describing my bad decisions, I hope to show that the self-serving, self-gratifying wide
road is always a dead end. I hope to save some from needless
pain. But the story does not end with myself. It goes on to tell
of God's incredible and surprising grace. Because I simply
trusted Him, He has stunned me by turning my pain into
purpose, my desperation into hope, my broken dreams into a
vision of His kingdom. Remarkably and supernaturally He
has restored my soul.

Yet even now, as my heart longs to follow God, I often find
myself wandering away from Him. In a thousand ways, pursuing a thousand subtle lies, I leave the narrow path, only to
return with a sense of desperation, pain, and emptiness.
Although hearing that might disappoint you, it is reality for
me and for every imperfect Christian I know.

The Bible says that we are to "encourage one another daily,
as long as it is called Today, so that none of you may be hard-
ened by sin's deceitfulness" (Heb. 3:13). As a man who has
traveled that appealing but destructive wide path, I hope this
book will encourage you to follow Jesus on the narrow road
to joy.

You will find the way to fulfillment and freedom in the pages
of this book. I know this because I copied the guidelines out of

another book—the Bible. They have always been there, but sometimes it's hard for us to see what is so plainly before us. Sometimes it takes being trapped and empty before we're willing to take another look at truth that has been there all along.

TWO

FALSE GODS

Lies Disguised As Truth

On the broad paths of destruction, the road signs are attractive: paradise just ahead. Food for the soul. Entering the state of bliss. The billboards, glittering in golden light, say: take, eat, enjoy, gather. The absence of speed limits and lack of yield signs promise excitement.

And although the messages are all lies, they are, in the words of Bruce Springsteen, "brilliant disguises." How can anything that looks so good, promises so much, and evokes such powerful longings be anything but right? Even if the messages are not entirely true, we rationalize, who cares as long as they work? It is easy to buy into lies without recognizing the true price: our souls.

I know. Early in my life I began to believe lies. I believed there were no consequences for moving away from God. I believed that pursuing pleasure now would not produce pain later. I believed I had to please myself since I couldn't please God. Even though my parents were devout and authentic Christians, I wanted *more* from life. I saw God as a dreadful and supernatural Being who had to be coaxed and manipulated into blessing. Yet I never left the church; I remained active. At the same time I tested the waters of the world. I was like a toddler pushing the boundaries of his parents' rules to see just how far I could go without getting in trouble. If I did this—say, get drunk with the guys after a high school football game—would God punish me? And then, when I got away with that, I felt more confident to try another sin. I would think, *See, I did that, and nothing terrible happened. No lightning bolts from heaven, no illnesses, no calamities.* It's too bad that God's consequences aren't always immediate.

In my heart I believed that God would never allow me to suffer irreversible damage, that He would reel me back in His great and harsh love before I had set a price on my soul. Before long, I was living with one foot in the church and one foot in the world. It was not unusual for me to sing a moving solo about God's love the morning after a night of riotous, prodigal-style living. I was surprised that God allowed me to get away with it. I mistakenly equated His silence with distance or inattention.

Desperate for acceptance and something to numb my pain and confusion, I sought to charm whomever I could. I relished being the life of the party, quick with a joke or glib comment that would make everyone smile. And to some extent, I was good at it. I won awards, friendships, praise, and promotions. Well into my young adult life, I believed the most deadly lie of all—that I was responsible for my own happiness.

TROUBLE IN PARADISE

In 1825, long before Hawaii met its first tourist, the U.S. schooner the *Dolphin* set out on a mission of justice. The captain was ordered to bring to trial a group of sailors who had led a mutiny on a ship called the *Globe*. The *Globe's* captain had had his head rather unceremoniously split in two with an ax. The mutineers, who settled on the island now known as Hawaii, believed they could live in that paradise without experiencing any negative consequences for their behavior. The crew of the *Dolphin* set out to prove them wrong.

What interests me in this story is not whether the mutineers were brought to justice or not (eventually they were), but the psychological drama that played out. When the *Globe* arrived on the shores of Hawaii, thousands of dark-skinned native people greeted the boats. For a while the crew feared for their lives since they were far outnumbered by the islanders. What would these island people do to the pale-skinned strangers? Because they were in desperate need of supplies, the crew decided to risk their lives by going ashore. Upon landing, an amazing thing happened: the native people began to treat the crewmembers like gods. In fact very little was required of them to gain worship. First, the islanders were impressed by the crew's fair skin, glimmering brass buttons, and ship with huge sails that harnessed the power of the wind. Second, the crew perpetrated a lie: they convinced the islanders that, although outnumbered, they could easily overpower them with super-natural force. The Hawaiians never once questioned the authority of the pale-skinned "gods."

Penned into a journal of the voyage that day was this profound entry: "So ready is the human mind to receive for truth, what it cannot comprehend . . . though it may be at variance with everything in nature or reason." I don't believe these crewmen possessed superior intelligence, but they had superior knowledge about the ways of the world. For them truth was simply a tool for power and control.

In the years that have passed since the voyage of the *Globe*, little has changed in the minds of men and women. Much of what is passed off as truth, or at least knowledge, is motivated by a desire to control and possess. Truth, then, is defined by abusive leaders as not so much a matter of what is "right or wrong" but what "works for me." Often we follow "truth" not because we are morally or spiritually convinced but because we are impressed by how many letters are behind the name of the "expert" who formulated the theory. We believe many so-called truths even though they may go against everything we've been taught.

We like to call ourselves sophisticates. We believe in scientific theory and read the *Wall Street Journal.* We subscribe to the theory, secretly or not, that mankind is evolving and that we are far superior to our brutish and superstitious ancestors. We smirk when we read how they worshiped gods—those deaf, dumb, and mute pieces of wood and gold. We scoff, *How could those people really bow down to a golden calf?*

Yet at the same time, without even knowing it, we are on our knees before more subtle (but just as real) false gods. They are the "isms" of our day: *workaholism,* as if the fruit of endless labors will finally bring satisfaction; *legalism,* as if being good and performing flawlessly will secure peace; *intellectualism,* as if we could get so smart that we would finally feel fulfilled; and *materialism,* as if some *thing* could give us joy.

The first step onto the broad path is to follow one of these false gods—lies brilliantly disguised as the truth, but lies nonetheless.

EMBRACED BY THE LIES

The most dangerous kind of lie comes clothed in the name of truth and sold as religion.

In one manner or another, all false gods use the time-tested formula of transforming lies into "truth" as a way to win trust. It is a formula for disaster as old as the serpent in the Garden. Each enticement away from God's narrow road and onto the broad path begins with the same words the serpent used: "Did

God really say . . . ?" (Gen. 3:1). To believe a lie, we must first stop believing the truth. More often than not, this deception is not a blatant dismissal of the truth but a subtle distortion of it. The most effective lie is often the one that travels the shortest distance from the truth.

This philosophy asks the question: "If God—this 'warm, embracing light'—were God of love, would He send anyone to hell? Did Jesus, who was so gentle, really say He was the *only* way to heaven?" The unspoken reply is, "Of course not." But God's truth is often a hard truth. He tells us that by ourselves we are helpless, hopeless, and doomed by our sin. Although God provides a way out of this dilemma, it is not by doing an end run around these hard realities. Jesus, too, experienced the hardness of God's truth on the cross. The sinless One took on sin for us. He asked us to pick up our crosses and follow Him on the narrow path.

False gods are appealing because they cast doubt on the hard realities. The hook always appeals to our selfish interests with a lie. "You will not surely die" were the serpent's next words (Gen. 3:4). We are offered a god who tells us the things we *want* to hear. The apostle Paul said it this way: "For the time will come when men will not put up with sound doctrine. Instead, to suit their own desires, they will gather around them a great number of teachers to say what their itching ears want to hear" (2 Tim. 4:3).

With the lure of false gods come three primary lies: (1) human beings are basically good; (2) God would never punish us;

and (3) we can, by our own efforts, be like God. It doesn't matter which god you follow, the lies say, because in the end that god will embrace you in the light of heaven. In essence there is no one true God, so you can live your life any way you choose. You can control your own destiny.

The same is true with all of the false gods of our age, whether they are in the form of materialism, hedonism, moralism, or any other philosophy. The first step in the worship of false gods is exchanging the truth for lies. Once truth is discarded, anything can be believed.

Isaiah, the Old Testament prophet, issued a powerful warning to those who turn people from the truth: "Woe to those who call evil good and good evil, who put darkness for light and light for darkness, who put bitter for sweet and sweet for bitter" (5:20). Truth, the false gods tell us, is relative—what's good for me may be bad for you and vice versa. In our age the worst thing you can be labeled is "intolerant." Yet relative truth, by its very nature, is an oxymoron. How can two opposing ideas be true? Either there is one absolute truth, or there is no truth at all.

The truth of the Bible does not change according to the situation or circumstances; it defines and weeds out all falsehood. And it is an uncomfortable truth that speaks hard things about the nature of reality, God, and people. Biblical truth maintains that only by the life and death of Jesus Christ can we receive salvation from God. We can do nothing through our own efforts, abilities, and power to save ourselves. We must accept these hard facts before the truth can ever set us free.

LIES ALONG THE NARROW PATH

Not only the self-proclaimed spiritual gurus, the heathen, and the power-hungry believe and practice the lies of the world. Some of the most dangerous truth twisting I know is done within what is supposed to be the body of Christ, the church. Claiming to lead us on the narrow path of truth, some of these people take us on dangerous, dead-end excursions.

There is a temptation for Christians to say it doesn't really matter what we do because grace covers us, and even if we are misled, we are still covered by Christ's blood. That is the beginning of the lie—in such a profound truth. It's essential to realize that anytime we leave the narrow path, we face death. Maybe not physical death but a death to the new life that God desires for us.

Within the church false teachers create a toxic faith. By departing from the hard truth (often quite subtly), they often cause the people they shepherd to lose their love for God and turn their backs on the church. Unfortunately many of us are too willing to believe whatever people tell us, especially if they claim to be doing the will of God. We read in the Bible that we must be "as shrewd as snakes" (Matt. 10:16). When it comes to believing what others say, we must be discerning and disciplined, filtering out the truth from lies.

One of the biggest lies within the body of Christ claims that once we accept Christ, our lives will be free from problems. Mirroring our society's quest for painless, instant results, some misguided teachers say that Jesus is the answer—and they stop there. They never mention the inevitable spiritual struggles and sacrifices necessary to live a God-honoring life. In a way people who teach struggle-free Christianity put a perverse spin on the lie that man is basically good. Although they concede it is Christ's blood that washes us clean, they do not give enough credence to the pervasive nature of sin, even after we accept Christ as Savior. Even the apostle Paul struggled with this issue, saying, "I have the desire to do what is good, but I cannot carry it out. For what I do is not the good I want to do; no, the evil I do not want to do—this I keep on doing" (Rom. 7:18–19). Paul understood the enormous power of sin.

Christianity doesn't promise that we will be free from the consequences of sin. In fact Christians, of all people, should be the most aware of its deadliness. Instead of ignoring sin or downplaying its effects, Christians must deal with it through the power of Christ and in the name of love. That means a continual struggle because the flesh will constantly be at odds with the spirit.

Those who promise a life without problems create problems. The flip side of the lie is this: if you struggle, there must be something wrong with your faith. This notion is a dangerous mockery of grace.

THE DIFFERENCE BETWEEN FREE AND CHEAP

The idea that God takes away all of our problems has more than one deadly offspring. If we don't fall into the trap of legalism, then we can be tempted to believe that God should be our personal Miracle Worker. The Bible says if we have enough faith, then God will answer our prayer. That is true. But the truth gets subtly twisted when we believe God has a *responsibility* to heal on demand, whether it is a broken relationship, a diseased body, or a shattered dream. If we do not receive healing, the reasoning goes, then there must be sin in our lives that prevents God from granting our request.

On my fiftieth birthday a couple who are wonderfully devoted Christians threw me a party. I love these people. Their first daughter was born with a severe mental disability that will force her to be dependent on her parents all her life. Their second child was born with a serious physical anomaly. These tragedies occurred despite many prayers by the parents and family members that God would give them healthy children. Some Christians had the audacity to tell them that their children were born that way because of sin in the parents' lives. Can you imagine the pain that those hurtful comments caused the already suffering couple?

The Bible clearly teaches that illness and physical maladies are not always the results of anyone's sin; they happen so the work of God can be manifested in a person's life (John 9:1–3). God is more interested in a person's faithfulness and maturity in the face of suffering than He is in preventing us from experiencing pain.

When we leave the path of God's truth, death always occurs. Sometimes, as our friends discovered, the death can be a loss of hope and trust in the community of Christ; other times it may be actual death. When I was conducting research for the book *Toxic Faith* back in the '90s, I discovered that more than 126 children had died over the previous few years because their parents withheld medical treatment, convinced that God would heal.[1] The sickness of their parents' beliefs led to these children's deaths every bit as much as their physical diseases did.

The story of Michael is a story of death but with an off twist. It is an example of a church that was full of love but was, at the same time, badly misled. Michael, a discharged patient from a mental institution, began attending a church in Orange County, California. Despite being labeled a schizophrenic, he developed relationships within the church and, for the first time in his life, felt genuinely loved and accepted. Soon he started doing odd jobs around the church. He became a Christian, and people learned to trust Michael.

Then one day a naive young pastor told Michael, "Now that you have become a Christian, you are a new creature in Christ. All of the old things have passed away, and all within you is new." He advised Michael to stop taking his medication, which he did. In a few days, tragedy struck. While he was babysitting the children of a woman in the church, Michael killed her three-year-old son.

Later, sitting in a jail cell being interviewed, Michael said, "When I drove a knife through that baby's heart, I felt the hand of Satan guiding my hand. I felt that I was Satan."

In a schizophrenic delusion he killed a child. What had been a wonderful story of restoration and healing suddenly turned into a nightmare for a young man, a family with a dead child, and a naive pastor who now says he will never again tell anyone not to take medication. Michael, once a thriving member of a church, now sits in prison. He will probably always be in an institution of some kind.[2]

We need to use our God-given brains and stop victimizing people, whether it is with quick fixes and instant solutions or shallow answers that rob people of their faith. We must realize that faith is a process and that struggle, doubt, and imperfection are not enemies of the gospel, but are often used by God to develop the faith He wants in each of us.

THE PERFECT-MATE MYTH

The lies of the world have also infiltrated the church in the area of relationships. We believe, in our hearts, in what I call the Perfect-Mate Myth. This belief, which applies to both singles and married couples, goes something like this: "If I just had the right mate, then my life would be alright." This belief is incredibly ignorant. First, it assumes that we are good and the spouse (or lack of a spouse) is the *real* problem. Second, it implies that there is such a thing as a "perfect" spouse, one who is beyond the reach of sin.

This delusion keeps people from growing the way God wants them to grow. For those in difficult marriages, it prevents them from the hard work and commitment necessary to repair the relationship. And singles can be tempted to keep life on hold until the "right" spouse comes riding into his or her life. In either case God is supposed to painlessly fix things by finally providing the right spouse. For God to ask us to stay and fix a marriage or for Him to deny us a spouse altogether seems cruel or unfair.

God is most concerned about our relationship with Him. If we are married, we will find that the way to keep the relationship stable and growing is to build our relationship with God—as a couple and as individuals. If we do that, our marriages will be strengthened along with our souls. God wants our attitude to be, "I'm in this for the long haul. I'm going to dedicate myself to making this marriage last." This is how an active and true faith comes alive in a marriage that will be anything but perfect or close to paradise. Similarly God wants the attitude of every faithful Christian single to be, "God, I'm Yours whether I have a spouse or not." Whatever your situation, God is sufficient to meet your needs.

GIVING TO GET

Our culture's emphasis on getting what is "ours" has created a dangerous attitude regarding service in the church. We sometimes serve because we expect to be blessed. Although Scripture promises that our lives will be fulfilled through serving God and one another, the truth has been subtly twisted— we expect our blessing as a *reward* or payment, not as a *gift*. There is a world of difference. One mind-set demands from God; the other gratefully accepts.

People who serve only to receive blessings operate more under the law than under grace. They produce good works, believing they will be compensated with blessings from God. Because such people operate under the serpent's lie that they are basically good, they focus on service as being good work that *should* be rewarded by God. They tend to forget that this same reasoning dictates that sin deserves consequences (punishment).

In many churches this belief is taken to an extreme in the area of financial giving. Many people are fed the lie that if they give their money to God, He will give them more in return. One church leader convinced his parishioners to give 100 percent of their salary each January as a way of honoring God with their firstfruits. In principle that may not sound bad, but he went on to promise that by doing so, all of those who gave would receive more of God's fruit in return throughout the year. Only in our materialistic age could we imagine that God wants us to have a lot of money, and therefore we should give Him a little and wait for Him to make us rich. Yet millions believe that if they have enough faith, God will reward them with financial blessings.[3] I wonder how many people have turned from Christ because their expectations were so out of line with reality.

THE FALSE GODS

Satan, the Bible tells us, is the father of lies. Lies are the foundation, the starting point of his strategy. With glittering deceptions his lies ask, "Did God really say . . . ?" Once we abandon truth, we open ourselves up for all kinds of lies. As we have seen, these lies tend to focus on the following: people are basically good; sin is not that bad; and people are more deserving of reward than of punishment.

When we operate under these false premises, we are no longer completely dependent upon God. His grace becomes something we can manipulate, buy, or charm. And when life does not turn out exactly as we hope, we fall into the most devious lie of all—that we, by our own effort, can control the destiny of our lives. We become our own false gods. It is here that inward faith is turned into superficial religion, that loving grace is transformed into deadly law.

THREE

MATERIALISM

The Desire to Acquire

I still remember the night. I was twelve years old, and my best friend and my girlfriend—or I should say the girl I *wished* was my girlfriend—were leaving for camp. I had to stay home. My parents said they just didn't have the money to send me. Later in life, I would understand that my brother, who was six years older than I, wanted to go to college, and my parents were simply exercising priorities. Yet I wailed in my bedroom, and I felt that my dad and mom were poor, poorer than anyone in our home state of Texas.

The night before I was to be left behind, I cried heavy tears all over the picture I wanted to give my "girlfriend." I didn't want her to forget me. They were going all the way to Branson, Missouri, to Camp Kanakuk for boys and Camp Kanakomo for girls. I couldn't afford to make the trip, but I felt as if I couldn't afford *not* to be there. I knew I could easily miss my opportunity with this girl.

The camp was more than just another dude ranch. It was the world to me. And it wasn't just that I wanted to go and have fun; I desperately wanted to fit in, to feel that I belonged somewhere. I didn't always feel that way at home. I was a sensitive child, and I knew my parents loved me, but some unhealthy dynamics were going on in my family. My dad, a man of deep faith who genuinely loved his children, was not raised by a father who taught him how to relate emotionally. My mother was the one primarily in charge of raising the children since my dad traveled a lot. But she was struggling to deal with the suicide of her father, which happened when I was a year old. She did her best, but she never had the opportunity at that time to work through her confusion and loss (which she has subsequently done).

So I searched for a place to belong. And that year, as I stood on the brink of entering a troubling adolescence, the place was a camp in Branson, Missouri. Because I did not get to go, one of my friends ended up being the one to kiss "my" girl. Combining that pain (a big deal at that age!) with the reason I couldn't go (my family couldn't afford it) reinforced a misconception that had taken root in my mind—money was something that could connect me to where I wanted to go and to who I wanted to be.

In retrospect I realize we were not as poor as I thought. My father owned three fast-food restaurants, and my mom owned and managed several beauty shops. We were certainly not wealthy, but my family's poverty was more in my mind than anything. I just always *felt* we were poor. None of us boys received an allowance, I had to wear hand-me-down clothes, and our family was rarely invited to the places that the "in" people went. Each year, for example, many of my friends' parents went to Padre Island for a Fourth of July week of fun and fireworks. Our family never was invited. Although the snub had more to do with the fact that my parents didn't drink alcohol (a main attraction of the week), I equated it with our financial condition. Worse, my less-than-mature mind made a fallacious spiritual connection: if God really loved me, I reasoned, He wouldn't want me to be a second-class citizen in a first-class world.

To hide my feelings of inadequacy and pain, I compensated by hanging out with people who looked successful and well-off. Deep down, I felt as if I could increase my worth by merely being in the presence of the successful. My first real girlfriend (after the other budding romance fizzled) was the daughter of a farmer who owned a significant amount of land. She was a delightful girl with many wonderful qualities, but my attraction started with her family's prosperity. My next girlfriend was also the daughter of a wealthy man in the area.

I was drawn to her father's outward signs of success long before I discovered just how remarkable she was as a person.

This set a pattern that continued well into my adult life—outward appearance was always at least as important as inward qualities, if not more important. I bought into the same lie that Hollywood and the Manhattan advertising agencies whisper, and sometimes scream, into our ears every day. I made decisions based on superficial rather than spiritual reasons.

My reactions were somewhat unusual. Often people who feel inadequate in a certain area seek out others who are even less adequate, hoping to look good by comparison. I did just the opposite. I hoped that by rubbing shoulders with the rich and successful, some good would rub off on me—or at least that people might think more highly of me for having influential connections.

Interestingly, my longing to succeed and attain material wealth did not prompt me to work hard to achieve it. My life during those years mirrored the title of the popular stage play *How to Succeed in Business Without Really Trying.* I was unmotivated, undisciplined, and hurting. In college I graduated with a degree in elementary education—certainly not in the Fortune 500 top 10 moneymaking degrees. I chose that major partly because I could not decide what else to do and partly because I knew it was a fairly easy degree to obtain. My attention deficit disorder kept me from learning a foreign language and, ironically, elementary education was the one place I didn't have to learn one. It was the only way for me to get a degree. I never thought of working harder or getting help because I just thought it would all fall in place for me. I kept one foot in the world, with its potential riches, and one foot in the church, storing up heavenly treasures "just in case." In the end I nearly split myself in two.

Although I always struggled with deep feelings of inadequacy, in truth I was gifted. That was a deadly combination. It kept me from discipline or repentance and left me feeling that I constantly had to perform. I could succeed without a great deal of effort. On the football field I was the starting fullback. In church I could knock the congregation out of the pews with my hard-driving solos. In school I could do well without cracking a book. People told me they expected me to do great things. On top of all that, I was a comedian.

But in those rootless early adult years, I soon discovered that I lacked what was necessary for real success—discipline and strong character. Even though I was buoyed by a scholarship and praise for my natural singing gifts, my dream of becoming a professional singer (musical comedy suited me) faded as soon as I ran into the walls of difficult theory and endless arpeggios. I quickly learned that I could not charm my way to success and riches. All the things I wanted so badly became elusive. I desperately desired what I couldn't have. Consequently I became even more ensnared in the trap of materialism.

Aside from my parents, whom I found myself resenting for their "poverty," I had no clear example of someone who was free from the power of money. Even my pastor, by example, taught me to choose money, power, and pleasure over the treasures of God's kingdom. Growing up, I attended a thriving Baptist church in which the pastor was experienced and educated, with a doctor of philosophy in theology degree—not a backwoods hick preacher. He had a Ph.D. behind his name, just in case anyone doubted that he knew, and had thoroughly studied the truth. Indeed, he won many people to Christ.

Eventually, however, this man did not look for meaning and significance in the truth of the Bible. He ended up leaving his wife and children to marry one of the church members, a recently widowed and extremely rich woman. In addition to deserting his family, the pastor abandoned our church, as if we were a cheap date and not the bride of Christ. His example deluded many church members, including me, about what really matters in this life.

LESSONS FROM A SALESMAN

Materialism has been a deep source of confusion for me. Even when I should have known better, and even when I was sincerely turning to God in faith, the pursuit of things has tripped me up. After college, which was a dreadful period of pain and numbness for me, I decided to go to seminary. I was broken and deeply repentant over my sin. I wanted to start over. Yet, once again, I fell into the trap of chasing after things.

Just before starting seminary, I bought my first house for $10,000 with a down payment of only $1,000. The monthly mortgage payment was $100. What a deal! I congratulated myself for being so financially astute. But a door-to-door salesman changed all that. He came one day selling carpet, which was my house's only real deficiency. Covering the floors was a harvest gold–colored carpet that, over the years, had turned into more of a harvest-dirt color. The salesman showed me a sample of sea-foam green, stain-resistant, nylon-and-polyester-blend carpet. I was hooked. I simply *had* to have it. It was the most beautiful piece of carpet I had ever seen.

I didn't have the money to pay for it, so the salesman arranged for me to have credit. Before he was finished, I had a home with brand-new wall-to-wall carpet and a payment coupon book about as thick as *Webster's Dictionary*—something like $35 a month for the next thirty-five years. Lovely. But there was another problem. After I had the beautiful new carpet installed, I noticed how ratty my furniture looked. A furniture sale quickly resolved that problem. I filled my house with a desert wildflower design. All I had to do was agree to pay $45 a month for forty-five years or something like that. But then there was another problem. As I was munching Doritos on my desert wildflower sofa, I realized how poor the reception was on my television. To remedy the situation, I bought a state-of-the-art Sony TV.

So there I was watching my new television on my new desert wildflower sofa, which sat on my new sea-foam green, stain-resistant, nylon-and-polyester carpet. From the desert to the sea, everything seemed perfect until the bills started rolling in, one after the other. Along with the other debts that I had accumulated, the new bills put me over the top. I couldn't make the minimum payments. For a while I fought off the creditors. In a panic I responded to an advertisement for a bill consolidation loan company. After filling out more forms than it takes to get into college and waiting longer than it takes for an IRS return, I was finally granted a loan. By pooling my debts and extending the payments until I was sure I would be a great-grandfather, I could make the minimum payment each month. *Eventually*—and I cannot stress the word enough—I was able to pay off all of my bills.

What I thought would bring me respect and comfort made me a slave. But I didn't find out the worst of it for years to come. I was simply dealing with the *symptom*—a desire to acquire—and not the underlying pain and emptiness that make things so attractive to me in the first place.

LOOKING GOOD VS. BEING GOOD

I could have blamed it on the culture. God knows we live in a society obsessed with things. We compete with one another to see who can acquire the most things, and then we measure ourselves—more surely than by our height and weight and IQ—by the size of our pile of stuff. Television, billboards, and blimps bombard us with the message that if we are to be truly successful, we must have things. Possessions, the brightly packaged lie says, are capable of granting us power, respect, acceptance, and safety. The sales pitches tap into deeply felt needs and make us squirm until we have acquired.

At a party I met a woman who told me about all the products she had purchased from late-night television infomercials. The array of goods was truly amazing; she had everything from sonic-powered toothbrushes to stain removers, fishing lures to food dehydrators, hair-cutting devices to contraptions that would produce rock-hard abs (in just five days!). Even though she was single, she had purchased numerous tapes and kits promising the secret to a lasting and happy marriage. She said she needed to prepare herself.

This woman simply could not (or rather *would* not) resist. After sitting through one of these slickly produced "documentaries," complete with personal testimonies from doctors, social experts, and ordinary folk whose lives had been changed by this particular product, she would grab her credit card and pick up the phone. Most of the stuff she didn't need and rarely used, but she kept buying. Her house became a shrine to the infomercial gods.

"They make it look so good, so vital," she told me. "After I watch one of those infomercials, I'm convinced I just can't get along without the product they're selling. I should know better, but somehow I just keep getting fooled."

It's easy to laugh. We could easily dismiss her with a silly title such as "Infomercial Queen" and pass her off as an oddity. But she is more like you and me than we might first suspect. We may not stay up late at night and order power paint sprayers, but don't we all do the same thing in a different way? Don't we all believe deep down that if we could just have it, we would be truly fulfilled or at least partially satisfied? Maybe it is a new computer, a new house, a new car, a new (and higher-paying) job, or a new wardrobe. And isn't it also true that a short period of time after you buy *it*, it is not enough and must be replaced by still another *it*?

The cycle of materialism always ends in some form of addiction. What we thought would free us ends up enslaving us. If we are trapped in materialism, we never own things; they own us. I know of a Christian doctor who bought a house with a pool. He had always dreamed of owning a pool, for both the pleasure and the status that it offered. But as he described it, the pool ceased to be just a thing; it became like some ravenous creature from a Stephen King novel. The pool made endless demands on this family's life: feed me chlorine; get that leaf out of here; remove that algae; buy me pool toys; patch that crack; change my chemistry. There were, in fact, several months when the family did not feel free to travel because of the pool. Within just a few years, he sold the house, primarily because he no longer wanted a pool.

"I knew that when I reached the age of seventy," he told a friend, "I didn't want to be best remembered for how clean I kept my pool."

What he had hoped would give his family pleasure and relaxation in the end turned into a demanding taskmaster.

So it is with many things we insist we cannot do without. Materialism trapped me into equating money and things with value. I longed to be connected with "quality" people, the movers and shakers, the "in" people, and although it was all leading me toward failure, I did find a way to achieve success. While attending seminary, I finally found my professional niche. Having experienced so many problems in my own life and having reconnected with God during my last year of college, I was able to help some people with their problems. I had become acquainted with a professional counselor, so I decided I wanted to get involved in counseling. Unlike myself in my earlier aimless years, I became motivated.

I took a job at a psychiatric hospital for highly disturbed people. I began two nights a week on the evening shift. I then moved to full-time evenings and then full-time days while I was pursuing a master's degree in counseling at the University of North Texas. Within two years I was the chief therapist at the hospital. Unfortunately the hospital was in danger of shutting down because it had trouble attracting enough patients. So I switched gears, to the business side of the hospital, working in public relations, media, and administration. The hospital experienced a remarkable turnaround.

Shortly thereafter, I was transferred to another hospital that the company owned in California. Two years after I completed my graduate school program and nine years after I had taken my first job as a patient attendant, I was named senior vice president of the company. I presided over one-third of the ownings of the company, which eventually made more than one-half of its profit. I was then hired away by another company, which was struggling to free itself from a pending bankruptcy, and my salary was doubled. At the age of thirty-two, I was chairman of a quarter-billion-dollar company.

On the surface I had broken through many of the barriers I'd felt during my childhood. Through hard work and good breaks, I had reached a level of success. Even though I truly desired a relationship with God, I placed great emphasis on appearances. I would wear Ralph Lauren Polo shirts—the ones with the little horse over the heart. I even owned a gold Rolex watch. For a long time I felt good in my shirts and watch. To some extent they defined who I was; they gave me a sense of power and control.

But somewhere along the way, something happened. I began to feel foolish. Those images of prosperity, which I had hoped would connect me with important people and give me a sense of belonging, left me feeling disconnected and broken. What I had long thought would bring fulfillment left me empty. I slowly became aware that instead of opening up relationships, those symbols of success actually separated me from others. In fact the whole purpose of those things was to build barriers between myself and other people. They became false readings of where I was in the world. They put me above others rather than with them.

I was presenting an image that, in my heart, I despised. I began to struggle against the hold of materialism on my life. For a long time I neglected the deeper issues of my heart, such as envy, disappointment, greed, and anger, which were driving my materialism. Although I eventually gave up the Polo shirts and gold watch, I left the envy in my heart mostly untouched; in essence, I dealt with materialism by hiding it—by driving a beat-up car or denying what I still wanted. But materialism, I found, can still have a strong hold on us, even if we live in virtual poverty. We can experience our lust just as easily in a shabby Volkswagen as in a shiny Lamborghini.

Materialism is one of the most deadly diseases I know. It can eat you alive at the very moment you think you look so good. When we acquire the outward trappings and the "ideal image," we often neglect the deeper issues of life—faith, character, integrity, and a desire to love God and others. We soon would rather *look* good than *be* good. In the end the things that we acquire can turn on us and threaten our souls. In Luke 9:25 Jesus asked His disciples, "What good is it for a man to gain the whole world, and yet lose or forfeit his very self?" I like to paraphrase that verse as, "It would be really stupid if you were to live your life gaining all the things the world has to offer and then lose your life forever. If the temporary things of this world separate you from the eternal God of heaven, you'd be a fool to spend your life pursuing those things."

Like many others who wandered through the opulent eighties, I was trapped in a cross fire—the deadly battleground of my heart. Painfully and slowly I had to learn that I needed to hold very loosely what I "owned." That wasn't—and still isn't—an easy thing for me to do. When I hold on to something I have cherished and long felt that I needed, I may loosen my grip only one painfully pried finger at a time.

FOUR

PLEASURE

Feel Good Now, Pay Later

Today my oldest daughter, Madeline, brings me some of my greatest joys. But shortly after she was born, Madeline's tears brought back my pain. I was simply unable to listen to her cry. Every time she cried, it was like a jagged saw ripping through my heart. I would do anything to stop her crying. I suppose by the time she was three months old, I would have spoiled her beyond any hope for recovery.

Friends and family suggested that I seek counseling. They suspected my distress and anxiety went beyond a new parent's response to a screaming baby. No stranger by then to the benefits of wise counsel, I agreed.

During one session, the Christian counselor and I were talking about the problem of the pain I felt when Madeline cried. He asked me to tell him my most significant memories of childhood.

"Some of my most vivid memories involve an old bathroom," I said.

I told him this with some hesitation because if you tell a psychologist that your most vivid memories took place in a bathroom, he might think, *Now we've really got something to work with!* Needless to say, my counselor's ears perked up.

The occasions early in my life centered on an old bathtub: the water was running, my mother was somewhere else, and I reached up and turned off the cold water. I literally watched the skin on my feet scald from the hot water. The same horror happened exactly the same way a short time later. It took me two times to realize that it wasn't a good thing to do.

In another incident I was standing on the toilet as someone dried me off; I slipped and my hand went down on an old gas heater that wasn't insulated. My whole hand became a blister. As my father rocked me to sleep, my hand throbbed in excruciating pain.

But my worst bathroom memory occurred when I was about a year old. I recall standing outside the bathroom with tears streaming down my face as I listened to my mother crying uncontrollably inside. I remember the deep sobbing sounds she made, as if her grief were so powerful that she could barely breathe. I felt the need for help—for her and for me. I stood outside the door with my hands above my head, trying to turn the doorknob.

My counselor suggested I ask my father about what was going on in my family at that time, which I knew was about the same time my grandfather died. When we talked, my father told me that my grandfather had not died of a heart attack as I had always been told. He had killed himself. To fight a severe depression, he had agreed to submit to electric shock therapy, which in those days ripped through the brain while the patient was wide-awake. The pain and terror must have been unimaginable. He vowed never to endure that again. For a while my grandfather was fine. Then slowly the depression overtook him again. Not wanting to face the electric shock therapy again, he chose a gun instead.

My mother wrestled with her father's death throughout my childhood. The stigma of a suicide in a Christian family was difficult for her. In addition to her deep grief, she struggled with the same depression that prompted her father's suicide.

The memory of my mom weeping inside an old bathroom, grieving her father's suicide, was a wound that hung over my childhood. My father said it took her six years to get over it, and in some ways I never did. That subconscious, emotional wound—and others like it that occurred throughout my childhood—I dragged into my adult life. I had to confront and leave behind those wounds I was too lazy to resolve in my early life or I would damage my own daughter with them. The Christian counselor helped me work through them. Christ freed me through that process. Now my girl's tears merely need to be dried; they do not signify for me a childhood obsessed with how to stop pain. They have taught me well.

FEEDING AN EMPTY EGO

As a young child, I knew the truth of God's Word, at least as well as any child can. My parents taught me the tenets of the Christian faith, both in word and in action. My father was actively engaged in developing and growing a church in Bryan, Texas, and my mother raised us with love, respect, and in the knowledge of the Lord. Like all parents, they were not perfect. My dad was sometimes distant and quiet; as a child, I never knew he struggled. My mom, of course, was fighting her own private battles while she tried to care for her children.

The mistakes I made were not my parents' fault. I made decisions that I knew were based on lies, or at least on the truth as I tried to reconstruct it. Because of my parents' insistence on keeping rules, I began to see God as a naysayer, a taskmaster, a great destroyer of fun and pleasure. Because I attempted so desperately to soothe the wounds of my childhood and adolescence, I had little or no concept of delayed gratification. My pain, I believed, needed immediate attention.

In seeking a quick fix, I hurt myself even more deeply. I wanted immediate pleasure. When my high school girlfriend, the light of my life, wouldn't consent to have sex, I found someone who would. Rumors followed. My girlfriend found out, and our relationship was over. I gave up a fairy-tale romance for a few moments of instant gratification. Worst of all, I hurt someone I really loved. I knew it, I felt it, and I hated the pain I had caused her. She stood for what was good, and I betrayed her with evil. I was surprised at just how deeply betrayal can hurt the betrayed and the betrayer. That incident had a powerful impact on my life, filling me with profound regret—irreversible regret that I attempted to medicate with more sinful pleasure.

It was not just the obvious sinful pleasures—such as sex, lewd music, drinking, and drugs—that enticed me. Pleasure for me became anything that fed my empty ego. For instance, I took pleasure in making my friends laugh. That's not unusual or wrong in itself, but I would go to almost any length for a big laugh. Once, after my father took his car into the shop for a buzzing noise, I retrieved it for him and drove it to the railroad tracks near our home. Five of my friends and I drove the car up on the tracks, where we revved the engine and spun the wheels until—*clank!*—it fell onto the railroad ties. We howled! (I guess you had to be there.) Slowly we placed it back on the tracks and drove away before a train slammed into us. Before the day was over, the buzzing noise, which had been repaired, returned. My father was furious at the mechanics for not fixing it.

Pleasure for me was singing a solo at church, in my best booming voice, and bringing people to tears over God's holiness. Pleasure for me was taking a handoff from the quarterback and slamming into the end zone for a winning touchdown. Pleasure for me was another award, certificate, or honor. Those things weren't bad in themselves, but my motives were.

Throughout those early years, my search for relief brought me some degree of respect, recognition, and power. I was considered popular, well-respected, and the life of the party. But I knew the truth about myself, and I was miserable. Even when I tried to earn back my self-respect, I fell deeper into sin.

In my heart of hearts, I knew the haunting truth—that I was the one who needed to change to fit the truth instead of trying to fit my life around a lie. I knew I had become obsessed with myself, my pain, my pleasure. I knew I had bought into the lie to look out for number one and pursue a life free of pain and full of fun. As time passed, the fun became more fleeting. I even longed to return to my faith and the truth, but I had no idea how to shed the unhealthy habits I had created.

I put a good deal of energy into dreaming. I performed and I collected accomplishments as if they were food for the soul. Eventually I stacked up my successes and shaped them into a dream, which in reality was more like an idol. My dream was to attend college, study music, and become the greatest musician in the world. Seriously. I would stop at nothing to pursue this dream. I knew if I could just make it happen, I would find true pleasure.

Ironically another pleasure got in the way. In college I dated a girl for whom I really cared. She was a Christian—bright, gentle, beautiful, and energetic. I believed we had a lot in common. Even though in my terrible spiritual condition, I mostly judged people on external appearances, I truly lucked out when I fell in love with her.

Because we loved each other, I had an easy time convincing her to sleep with me. I justified my sin—and hers—by believing that love covered everything. Yet, I discovered it was less love for her and more love for myself that led me to seek sexual gratification. How shameful that I didn't see what I was doing until it was too late. She missed one period, and then she missed another. She was pregnant.

Although I loved my girlfriend, I selfishly did not want to shatter my dream. At all costs I had to protect the only thing I thought could save me. Never once did I consider any options. Never once did I drop down on my knees and seek God's forgiveness and ask Him to show me a responsible way out of the problem. Never once did I doubt what had to be done. She had to have an abortion.

I was deeply immersed in the philosophy of the world. If something is inconvenient—say, a broken radio, a bad marriage, or a baby—just get rid of it. So there we were, my girlfriend and I and the baby growing in her womb. I carefully laid out my plan with all the details already put together: go here at such and such a time, they will do such and such to you, and then it will be over. We can go on with our lives. I'll even pay half the cost of the procedure.

My heartless and unbending pragmatism overwhelmed her. I never really gave her an opportunity to respond. No unwanted baby was going to stand in the way of *my* musical career. So she went because I convinced her it was the best way out of a bad situation and because she thought I loved her.

She and I would have a thirty-seven-year-old daughter today, and probably a few grandkids if I had not moved to take that life away. The guilt, shame, and remorse had emotional, physical, and spiritual consequences that had such a devastating effect on me that I almost lost my life.

THE BLIND LEADING THE BLIND

The summer after the abortion, I stayed with my brother Jerry in Easley, South Carolina. I killed time in a series of vacuous relationships with girls. Although I worked hard at having fun, it seemed that nothing could give me pleasure anymore. In the meantime Jerry was having trouble of his own (which I'll discuss in the next chapter). Truly, when it came to helping each other, it was the blind leading the blind. The prodigals were headed for the pigsty.

I returned home worse than when I left. The sex, drinking, and admiration had failed me, and the effects of the abortion began to surface. Only twenty years old, I fell into a deep depression, went on antidepressants, and began to feel as old as a grandfather. Within six months of asking my girlfriend to have an abortion, I was diagnosed with eighty-three ulcers. My doctor told me that I would have to make some serious lifestyle changes or have part of my intestines or my colon removed. Within a year I had dropped out of my music major and abandoned my dream. At the time I had no idea what was causing me such misery. I couldn't recognize the negative repercussions of my behavior. The consequences of sin did, indeed, appear to me—just not as quickly as I first thought they might.

SETTLING FOR LESS

I had fallen into the trap of demanding instant solutions. And why not? I lived in the world of technology as savior—instant banks, instant credit, instant coffee, and fast food. We pace in front of our microwaves. There is an irony here. When we demand instant fulfillment, we short-circuit the way God has made us. It is not as I believed—God was not intent on squashing all pleasure; in fact, He has wired us for intense joy. C. S. Lewis once wrote that God wants to give us pleasure, but we spend our time playing in mud puddles when He is offering us a cruise ship on the Caribbean Sea.

For instance, God created sexual passion. If He had been interested only in propagation, He could have designed a baby button, and the husband could have turned it on at night as he might a light switch. But sex, in God's wonderful and creative design, is to be more than just a way to make babies. It is a phenomenal way of showing love and intimacy with another person. The two shall become one.

Mankind has tampered with God's plan for sexual pleasure. Outside the lifelong bond of a loving marriage, sex becomes less human. Our society has not made sex free but has cheapened it. If you try to make sex "casual," "safe," and merely pleasurable, it will become destructive and demeaning. I imagine that God weeps when He sees His gift so degraded.

As Christians, we must rethink our image of God. Instead of being like the God of *Saturday Night Live*'s Church Lady, with lips puckered in prudish disdain of pleasure, our God is a progressive fun lover of passion and pleasure. He wants what is truly best for us. Yet at the same time, He hates it when we experience less than what He has designed for us. He hates it when sex becomes a toy, good for a thrill or a laugh, and then is tossed away like a paper plate. He hates it when His eternal and sustaining love is sacrificed for a twin-cam Sea Ray boat or a promotion to vice president of a company. He hates it when pleasure is confused with a numbing thrill.

When we discard the truth of the Bible, we are not, as we so smugly think, throwing away an outdated, stern, irrelevant book. On the contrary we are casting out our only real hope of deep fulfillment and lasting pleasure.

Rather than line up their behavior with Scripture, people often try to bring Scripture in line with their behavior. They write off the Bible as a book with no practical, modern application, saying, "This book is too old-fashioned," or "It was written for another day when they just didn't understand things the way we do." To accept the truth of the Bible would be to accept the need to submit to God, and that is one thing too many people are not prepared to do. As the apostle Paul wrote in Romans, "They exchanged the truth of God for a lie" (1:25). And without truth, there are always consequences.

A woman called the counseling program I cohost. She was completely miserable. The only times in her life when she felt power and meaning were when she was in the backseat of a car with a married man. Although she hungered for those times, she knew that she was destroying herself as well as the men with whom she chose to have affairs. When the counselor asked her what she thought she could do to develop a deeper level of purpose in her life, she responded, "Help other people in some way. Do some charity work." Even though the woman was far down the path of sexual addiction, she knew instinctively that what she was doing—pursuing self-interests—was wrong. She was confusing real pleasure with what made her feel *good* instead of choosing what made her feel *right*.

I understand this woman's misery. I, too, had aggravated my wounds by indulging in pleasures disconnected from God and His truth. I had created my own suffering. I can still remember the enormous emptiness and hurt I felt as I returned to school that fall after my girlfriend had the abortion. My body was racked with ulcers, literally bleeding into itself. My mind was tormented with doubts. My soul writhed in guilt. I had no clue about what I wanted to do with my life, and I had no one to turn to. That was where my life of pleasure seeking had led me.

Fortunately I came to an end of myself. In my desperation I was able to acknowledge that I had made a complete mess of my life and that I needed God's forgiveness and strength. I turned back to the narrow path. And even though I found God's surprising grace there, I also discovered that I had done enormous damage to myself. Because of sin, the path was overgrown with thorns and weeds. To this day, I still suffer some consequences of my sin. The roots of the world's thorn bushes and weeds grow very deep. I'm still tugging at some that refuse to be pulled up.

We all have wounds that never seem to heal—from childhood, from our sinful behavior, from living in the world. But the answer is not to pretend that they don't exist or believe the world's lie that we can alleviate them with self-gratifying pleasures. We must face our wounds honestly, repent before God, and let Him surprise us with His amazing and healing grace. It is only then that we can begin to experience what God has intended and desired for us all along.

FIVE

POWER AND CONTROL

The Seduction of Self-Sufficiency

I n the fall of 1984, we buried my other grandfather, my dad's dad, Art. We had gathered in Ranger, Texas, to pay our last respects. On that sunny, windy, and sad day, red dust blew around the cemetery, stinging our faces as we watched our grandfather disappear into the ground. My brother Terry delivered the eulogy.

That day, the hint of death was everywhere. My other brother Jerry was supposed to be a pallbearer, but he had come to me and said that he couldn't sustain the weight of the casket. Six months earlier, he had suffered a serious bout of pneumonia, and he still had not regained his strength. That surprised me, since Jerry was always as tough as steel, the model of vigor and resilience. I looked at him with concern and suspicion as my mind flashed back to another conversation we'd had several years earlier.

At that time we were having dinner with one of his friends in a California restaurant and began arguing about homosexuality. We continued our discussion as we paid our bill and walked outside.

"The Bible has been misinterpreted by people who condemn the gay lifestyle," Jerry protested as we faced each other in the restaurant parking lot. "It's just one of those gray areas. You can use the Bible to argue both sides of the issue."

"I disagree with you, Jerry," I told him. "I think the Bible is perfectly clear on that issue. But if you ever told me you're homosexual, you would still be my brother and I would still love you."

It was then that he first admitted to me that he was homosexual. We talked a bit more, reasonably and calmly, and then we parted. But as I drove away, my composure vanished, and I lost control.

I pounded the steering wheel and shouted, "Unbelievable! My brother—homosexual!"

I did not want to accept that my brother—a strong, popular, moral person, whom all the girls wanted to date—was homosexual.

And now, facing him at the funeral, I instinctively sensed

that my brother had AIDS. A knot formed in my stomach as I realized that in just a few years, I could be attending his funeral. He must have been thinking the same thing.

During the summer after I asked my girlfriend to have an abortion, I really got to know my brother Jerry. It was the summer of the Watergate trials, and the nation was disillusioned. So was I. It was an awful time in my life. Not only was I dealing with the guilt and shame over my girlfriend's abortion, but I had run a stop sign and smashed into a car, causing serious damage. A couple of people received minor injuries. They had threatened to sue, which did nothing for my already gnawing ulcers. I needed a place to escape, and my best option was Easley, South Carolina, where my brother was working as an administrator of a downtown renewal project.

Jerry put in a lot of hours at work. I put in a lot of hours with the opposite sex. From the time I arrived, I dated nearly nonstop, keeping myself so busy that I didn't have to confront the desperation I was feeling. I thought that if I just tried hard enough, I could regain some sense of control over my life.

I didn't know it at the time, but Jerry was doing no better than I was. He was also running from the hurt and insecurity in his life, trying to hide behind an image—his career, his reputation at church, and the "right" friends. He had a knack for success. But underneath his polished exterior, his deadly secret simmered in a poisonous soup of insecurity, pain, and emptiness.

Later I'd learn that Jerry had been sexually abused by one of the older boys at a church camp when he was five years old.

That experience, combined with having a father who was busy and often emotionally distant, formed in Jerry a powerful desire to please other men and win their approval. Most of this desire, he said, was not sexual but a desperate attempt to gain attention and acceptance. For the most part, he controlled his infatuation with men by pretending it didn't exist. But as that increasingly failed, he tried to cover it up with a gold-plated image. Like me, Jerry defined himself by exteriors.

It was during that same summer that my brother had his first homosexual experience. After midnight, in a swimming pool, another man locked his legs around Jerry's waist as they hung from the diving board. It ended there, but it was enough to open a floodgate of emotion that swamped Jerry's carefully constructed defenses. I should have noticed his confusion and distress, but I, too, was drowning in a pool of pain.

Creating Ourselves in Our Own Image

Shirley MacLaine, the guru of New Age channeling, says that each of us has the power to be a god. What's more, she says that each of us *is* God. The only problem is, MacLaine contends, some of us don't know that we're God. So once we know we're God and start acting like Him, then we will find the fulfillment of being God.

Like Adam and Eve in the Garden, we are all tempted to believe this grand lie. We all want to be like God, to control our own destinies. With this subtle form of idolatry, we place our goals and aspirations above God, which in turn suppresses God's ability to guide us and use us as He chooses. Let me be clear. I am not saying that all of our plans and goals are selfish attempts to grab power for ourselves. After all, God gave each of us brains to use and gifts to employ as we strive to make our time on the earth count for something. But we must submit our desires and aspirations to God and be ready to alter our course according to His will and leading. As Proverbs 16:3 affirms, "Commit to the LORD whatever you do, and your plans will succeed." When we forget about God in the pursuit of our whims, we risk making our endeavors into idols. I love the imagery of Psalm 115:4–8, which speaks of the consequences of constructing idols in our lives:

> Their idols are silver and gold, made by the hands of men. They have mouths, but cannot speak, eyes, but they cannot see; they have ears, but cannot hear, noses, but they cannot smell; they have hands, but cannot feel, feet, but they cannot walk; nor can they utter a sound with their throats. Those who make them will be like them, and so will all who trust in them.

Of course, you and I are too sophisticated and progressive to worship statues fashioned of gold, bronze, or wood. That would be too blatant, too flagrant. So we ever so subtly shift ourselves to center stage, putting our desires and goals into the spotlight and ahead of everything else. We begin to create ourselves in our own image. In a sense we make ourselves gods.

Some people are better than others at creating good-looking images. Since an image depends upon external comparison, there will always be some haves and some have-nots. And in the tension between those with and those without comes strife, conflict, and opposition—sometimes even violence and destruction.

Over the past few years we have seen wars and massacres in places such as Haiti, Rwanda, and Bosnia. Atrocities have occurred there and in hundreds of other places in the world because some people are power-hungry. They want influence and position for themselves, and they are willing to hurt anyone to achieve it.

Other battles for power and control are far more subtle. Perhaps it is a ladder-climber at the office who tramples on a coworker's good name to get a promotion and the corner office. Or maybe it is a president of a large organization who uses fear and intimidation to maximize his employees' productivity and build his empire. Or maybe it is a Christian woman, firmly self-righteous, who *knows* she could run the outreach program better than the current leader—and lets everybody know it.

We often hoard power, position, time, and prestige, thinking that if we gather enough, we will finally feel better about ourselves. But there is a serious catch to this plan: we can never obtain enough power or control to make our idols, our images, live. They are dead, worthless, hollow. They have not even a hint of life.

In a sudden twist, Psalm 115:8 warns us, "Those who make them will be like them, and so will all who trust in them." With a psychological and spiritual insight second to none, the Bible states that the idols we create—those lifeless, external objects of worship—will not only fail to deliver, but they will actually kill us in the process. By trying to take total control of our lives, we damage our souls.

When control becomes our mode of thinking and acting, we will sooner or later begin to treat people like things. When I realized I was doing this with people on our New Life Clinics staff, it was quite a shock. I, a great lover of people, had become a user of people. I had to get away, breach the pattern, and restore the love I had lost.

Many parents control their children in one way or another. Some are strict disciplinarians who care more about how their children appear to others than they do about developing genuine character. Having had their own dreams dashed, some parents live vicariously through their children, pushing them to excel in gymnastics or music against their wishes.

Control often occurs in marriage too. What about the husband who tries to control his wife? He may quote Scripture at her, but he actually wants her to become submissive or more like him so he will like her better. Instead of creating the loving environment necessary for her to fulfill her God-given potential, he demands that she change and see things his way. He fashions an idol in the distorted image of his own self.

In my life I had to hit bottom before I could admit that I

was ignoring God and trying to control my own destiny. I realized that I could not play the game anymore. No matter how
hard I tried, I could no longer work up the energy or the desire
to continue on the path that had brought me so much pain.
For once I could not act or perform my way out of a situation.
The only real option was to confess my sin before God and
rely on His sustaining grace as I walked painfully through the
consequences of my mistakes.

GRABBING CONTROL VS.
REFUSING RESPONSIBILITY

Our society encourages us to focus on ourselves. We prize indi-
vidualism and autonomy, often at the expense of community
and cooperation. We love the loners, the John Waynes and Clint
Eastwoods, who follow their own rules and don't take guff from
anyone. Advertisements tell us to indulge ourselves because "you
deserve it." The courts focus on individual rights, and as a result,
our country and communities have suffered deep divisions. As
individuals, we believe it is our "right" to pursue happiness.

The need for control is a disease with many symptoms. It can
be quite blatant and aggressive. I heard a tape by G. Gordon
Liddy, who was part of the Nixon administration during
Watergate and is now a successful talk show host. Most of his
life story is a testimony to the power of self. In his book *Will,* he
describes how he would go to almost any length to keep control
over his life. His particular lifelong battle was with fear.

Rather than run from fear, Liddy stared it down. To conquer his fear of electricity, for example, Liddy crawled up a telephone pole until he was so close to the high-intensity wire that his hair stood on end. But Liddy held on, and afterward he was no longer afraid of electricity. Another time, to conquer his fear of rats, he captured one, killed it, and cooked its haunches for his lunch. He never feared rats again. Liddy was committed to the theory of control. He was the ultimate in tough-guy, I-don't-need-anyone self-sufficiency. Even after his arrest and imprisonment for masterminding the Watergate break-in, he remained firm in his resolve, in the power of his own will.

Once, Chuck Colson, a fellow conspirator in the cover-up and then a new Christian, approached Liddy in his jail cell. He asked, "Mr. Liddy, have you seen the light?"

"Mr. Colson," Liddy replied, "I'm not even looking for the switch."

In contrast to Liddy's aggressive pursuit of control, others take a defensive approach. Instead of overcoming, they allow themselves to be overcome. At no point in our country's history has there been such an epidemic of "victims"—people who have declared themselves powerless against their circumstances, genes, metabolism, or upbringing. Rather than seeing his vulnerability and protecting himself, the alcoholic says, "Drinking problems run in my family—it's genetic. There's nothing I can do about it." The criminal says, "It's not my fault that I steal. I had lousy parents who didn't teach me any better." Our culture hands out excuses like ATM machines dispense cash.

I am not saying that our circumstances, genes, and upbringing do not affect who we are. But we are responsible for our own behavior. With the help of God, all of us are capable of change. Sometimes people allow their lives to self-destruct simply so they can play the helpless role of victim or martyr. I frequently see people who create or allow circumstances to develop that destroy them. Some people accumulate heavy debt, or flounder in a bad job, or refuse to resolve negative relationships. Instead of taking responsibility for their lives, they allow them to crumble, and then, they fall back on excuses, such as bad luck, bad genes, or bad parents. Christians often find an excuse to ask God for a miracle or to raise an angry, clenched fist at Him. The power in such victim mentality is that we never have to blame ourselves. It is always someone else's fault—our boss, our God, our friends, the Trilateral Commission, the liberal Democrats. The problems are anybody's fault but our own.

My brother Jerry fell into this trap. Wrestling with his homosexual behavior, he became angry at God for "giving him" homosexual feelings. He prayed diligently and fervently for God to take away the feelings. Yet, he did little to remove himself from circumstances that might prompt those same feelings. In essence he wanted change without facing the pain that comes with it. Jerry tried the best he knew how. On more than one occasion, he tried to escape the homosexual world; once, he lasted a year. But he always returned when the pain became too great. He craved the attention and acceptance the gay lifestyle offered, and he was unwilling to honestly face the deeper issues in his life. Jerry was sincere, but he lacked the accountability and understanding to make his commitment stick. He discovered that you can't leave one way of life unless you enter another one full of support and healthy relationships.

Finally Jerry's choices caught up with him. In April 1985, while hospitalized with a bout of pneumonia, he was diagnosed with AIDS. The suspicions I'd had at our grandfather's funeral were confirmed. Jerry tried to live in secrecy for a year and a half, but eventually he was forced to disclose his condition or face death alone. His first step was to acknowledge his homosexuality as sin. In his book *How Will I Tell My Mother?* he wrote, "What does come from it [homosexuality] is a complete destruction of mind, body, spirit, and the inability to utilize God-given talents to accomplish great things for His glory." Although he was specifically referring to homosexuality, his description certainly applies to sin in general.

After repenting of his wrongdoing, Jerry sought our family's forgiveness, which was extended to him in unconditional love. He then determined to make the rest of his life count for God, no matter how long that might be. He wrote, "I told God that He had my body, mind, and soul. I was done, and I was played out." He entered counseling to begin to understand the underlying issues in his life. As he was freed from his self, he began to serve others. He ministered to people dying of AIDS in hospitals and care facilities, many of whom had been abandoned by family and friends. Though he was gaunt, disabled, and nearly breathless from the ravaging disease, Jerry finally felt a deep sense of wholeness in his soul.

It was supposed to be a joke. G. Gordon Liddy, appearing on David Letterman's show, tossed off the comment as casually as a fisherman tosses old bait. In response to the question, "What happens when you die?" Liddy responded, "Worm meat. Eventually the coffin disintegrates in the ground, and you become food for worms. That is where it all ends."

For years, this punch line soured in Liddy's soul. There had to be a difference between funny and tragic. A purposeless life was tragic, not funny. Finally Liddy, the king of self-sufficiency, surrendered control of his life to God. "Not my will," he prayed, "but Your will." God surprised even the strongest of wills. I don't know where Mr. Liddy is today in his walk with God. But I do know that a man with an unusually strong will came face-to-face with himself and surrendered—as my dying brother did—to the power and control of the Creator.

On June 13, 1988—almost three years after his diagnosis—Jerry Arterburn died due to complications of the AIDS virus. His funeral, though not without grief, was a celebration. He died feeling the joy that comes when we relinquish control of our lives to God. Those who attended the funeral were struck by the contrast between what we do to ourselves when we take control and what God can do when we surrender to His power.

PART TWO

A SOUL RESTORED

SIX

THE PATH LESS CHOSEN

One Way to Restoration

I remember the trip as if it were yesterday. It was October of 1973, and I was in my car driving home from a seminar on youth conflicts. My parents had signed me up, and I was so desperate to find solutions to my messed-up life that I agreed to attend. Strange things had been going on in my heart, rumblings that I had not known for a long time. In one sense I was giving up some things; in another sense I was being stripped of them. At the seminar I had made a list of all the people I had hurt through my sins— my reckless self-seeking—in order to write to them or call them later to ask their forgiveness. It was an incredibly painful act that provided an unexpected and enormous sense of relief.

In the car I grabbed a pack of cigarettes and shredded them. I remember my violence spread tobacco over the car like a pod of seeds cast by a strong wind. I had wanted to quit not only smoking but also all of the self-destructive habits I had adopted. I was exhausted, broken, and desperate enough to believe that I could begin again. In the darkness I prayed, *Help, Lord. Give me a second chance.* That was the gist of it. I was determined to trust in God and not myself.

As I drove, I felt an overwhelming sense of forgiveness, relief, hope, and euphoria all at once. Never before or after have I felt so overwhelmed by God. The Lord's presence was so strong that He might have been sitting in the passenger seat of my Oldsmobile. For the first time in my life, I truly gave control over to God. Even though I didn't have a clue about what the future held, I was less anxious than at any other time. I was certain of nothing but this: God had my life and soul in His hands, and He loved me.

What a strange ride! With tobacco strewn throughout the car, my dreams scattered, and my body riddled with ulcers, I experienced perfect peace. Struck with flashes of understanding, I marveled at the sense of freedom I could have by simply trusting in God. I realized for the first time that I didn't have to manipulate and manufacture to make my life happen. As I gave control of my life over to God, truly trusting in His loving promises to meet my needs, I experienced a profound sense of security that comes only from complete surrender.

The sense of emptiness vanished. I understood that my mad searches for power, position, and prestige—attempts to control my destiny—were elusive. Like an alcoholic tired of trusting in the seemingly magical power of the bottle, I had reached the end of myself. I knew the only way to recover my soul was to admit that I was completely powerless. Only then could I find the healing power of God.

In some ways my life changed dramatically after that ride home. I picked up my rarely used Bible and began to read and study the Scriptures. For a long time I was overwhelmed with the words of God. It seemed that each time I read a verse, I heard the voice of God speaking directly to me. I still have that Bible, and every once in a while I look through it. The margins are full of notes and insights that God gave me.

As much as I'd like to say that everything got better overnight, I can't. My ulcers didn't miraculously disappear. For months I endured slow and painful healing. The guilt over my girlfriend's abortion didn't vanish into thin air. Years later, I was still uncovering the deep wounds caused by that experience. I still struggled with lust, materialism, and feelings of inadequacy. I still didn't know what God wanted me to do with my life.

In many ways my pain *increased.* Part of the reason was that I had truly repented; I realized just how destructive and hurtful my sins were to myself and others. I knew of the widespread consequences of sin, that the repercussions can continue even after you're restored to God. But probably the biggest part of my pain stemmed from my desire to keep secrets. I believed that the restoration of my soul was a project that God and I could handle alone, without help from anyone else.

I did not seek the understanding and accountability of others in the body of Christ. To admit that I had problems would have meant revealing my sin to others. I wanted to reveal only God's holiness and character as He worked in my life—and not the sinfulness and depravity He was rooting out of my heart. I didn't understand then that part of the transformation process involves vulnerability and accountability with a community of fellow believers. We are to tell and show each other the truth of our lives—the holiness *and* the sin—so that we can shine God's light, His Word, into the world.

Choosing to keep my struggles and inner conflicts to myself, I tried to get back on God's narrow path and serve Him with my life. I decided to go to seminary after graduating college. About the same time, I met a young woman and soon fell in love with her. But I did not understand the deeper issues in my life, and I failed to see what was really happening in the relationship. It was a one-sided relationship. As it turned out, she was not really in love with me, but perhaps she saw marriage as a better alternative to being alone. We married in 1975, but the relationship quickly unraveled. Just a few months into seminary and less than a year into our marriage, she left. I told my professors what happened, even though I knew the school's policy: anyone going through a divorce had to sit out a year. So that's what I did. That was an incredibly painful period in my life. I was confused because I had decided to serve God, which was why I had initially enrolled in seminary. Why would God block my path to serve Him? After all, I had been trying to live for Him for three years at that point.

Like my grandfather before me, I wrestled with suicidal thoughts. I simply did not know which way to turn. Even then, though, God had His hand on my life. As I mentioned before, I took a job as an aide in a psychiatric hospital for highly disturbed people, which soon led to my career in counseling. I learned the importance of honestly sharing and revealing thoughts, feelings, and tightly held secrets, so they can be brought into the light, wrestled over, and finally resolved. Secrets are, I believe, emotional and spiritual waste.

THE VALUE OF OPENNESS

From a biblical perspective, keeping secrets is wrong. Secrets are almost always rooted in sin. When we keep secrets in our hearts, then past sins and unresolved issues are allowed to fester, eating away at the soul and destroying our God-given potential. In many places the Bible tells us to share our burdens with one another and speak the truth to one another. And we should do so for a number of beneficial reasons. For example, the apostle Paul wrote about the purpose of the body of Christ and said that each of us should . . .

prepare God's people for works of service, so that the body of
Christ may be built up until we all reach unity in faith and in
the knowledge of the Son of God and become mature, attaining to the whole measure of the fullness of Christ. Then we
will no longer be infants, tossed back and forth by the waves,
and blown here and there by every wind of teaching and by the
cunning and craftiness of men in their deceitful scheming.
Instead, speaking the truth in love, we will in all things grow
up into him who is the Head, that is, Christ. (Eph. 4:12–15)

Paul was saying that each of us should speak the truth so
that we can reach full maturity in Christ, so that we can be
fully prepared to serve God. In my life I was harboring dark
secrets of paralyzing sin. The sin was connected to underlying
and unresolved issues that drove me to look to places and
things other than God for temporary relief. Because I didn't
want to hear the truth, I remained immature in my faith and
restricted in my ability to serve. My secrets were eating away
at my soul.

Most of us would like to pretend that deep secrets in our
lives don't exist. We would rather do anything than face the
inevitable pain that comes from looking closely at our own
souls.

As Christians, we have a profound responsibility to be honest with one another. We must both speak and listen—speak
about problems and hurts inside us, and listen to the problems
and hurts of others. It is only then that true healing can begin.

TURNING PAIN INTO PURPOSE

Up until this point in this book, I have described how my life became bankrupt because I listened to the lies of the world. But remarkably God turned my pain into purpose, and my soul is now truly learning how to live, to feed on the love of God. And that is the focus of the next several chapters—how the God of second chances restores our shattered lives and souls.

My journey of restoration would have been stalled if I had not learned to be honest and open with Him and with fellow Christians. I'm not saying that we should share our most deep and intimate secrets at a church potluck. There are appropriate and inappropriate times to reveal ourselves to others. Vulnerability without the walls of trust is simply a form of exhibitionism. Still, all Christians need someone in their lives with whom they can share what is really going on inside. Whether it is your spouse, a trusted friend, a small group, a pastor, or a Christian counselor, there *must* be at least one person who knows the truth about you. The process of healing begins when you *admit* there is something that needs to be healed.

I'm not going to lie to you. If you've gotten off course and followed the wide road, then getting back to the narrow path will be painful. It was for me. As I look back on the process of how God turned my life around, I realize that with almost every good gift came a challenge. My career is a good example. At the age of thirty-two, I was chairman of a quarter-billion-dollar company. A year later, I had a trustee appointed for the near bankrupt company, and I went in search of another job. The previous chairman had made some mistakes. There was no money for operations, and I had no way to fix things.

As I sought God's will, though, another "miracle" happened. A person who had followed my career with some interest approached me after hearing that the company I was working for went bankrupt. He asked, "If you had the money to start any company you wanted, what would you do?" I told him my dream of starting Christian counseling centers so that people could begin to tap into the healing power of God. This man's partner was a Christian, and both became excited about the idea. Within a few months, he had raised more than $2 million. In November 1988, we started the New Life Treatment Centers. But as exciting as that prospect was, it occurred during a time when counseling agencies and psychiatric companies were bottoming out financially. It was almost as if God were saying, "I'm going to give you the dream of your heart, but you'll have to trust Me with it." I believe that He knows my tendency to fashion even good things into idols.

But all was not good. My marriage was also a great challenge. As an infertile couple, we had little hope, having gone through the fertility rights of the medical profession. So while in the midst of God allowing me to start New Life, there were those who tried to take away the joy by suggesting we were childless because God was punishing me for my girlfriend's abortion years earlier. But God, far from wanting to punish me, had greater things in store for us. He allowed us to adopt a wonderful little girl, and now it is impossible to imagine my life without sweet and strong and loving Madeline.

God does not have a giant roulette wheel in the sky that determines our destiny. He brings events and circumstances into our lives that cause growth and maturity. God will certainly give us what we need, but what He most wants to give us is Himself. He longs for each one of us to be in a loving relationship with Him.

As God restores the soul, He also purifies desires. He wants us to stop taking detours into the world's glittering paths of possessions, power, and pleasure. Instead, He wants us to stay on course and continue to move toward Him.

The narrow path leads us to Living Water, pure and deeply satisfying for our thirsty souls. I know. Even though the refining process has been painful, I have found that knowing God is the only thing in the world that I truly desire. When my heart is right with God, all of my other joys come naturally through worshiping Him.

FAITH THAT WILL NOT LET US DOWN

When I was a boy, my family lived in a house with a creek behind it. Being young, I didn't realize that frozen creeks could be dangerous. One day I tried to cross on the ice, and I fell through and into the freezing water below. My little overcoat froze, and I thought my mom would have to use an ice pick to remove it from me. I had unwisely put faith in that thin ice, and I broke through it. I didn't understand that the flowing water underneath prevented the ice from thickening.

Later on that same day, my brothers took me to a frozen pond behind a field near our house. Since the water wasn't running, the ice was frozen thick and solid. Yet even when my brothers would run on the ice to demonstrate its sturdiness, they had a difficult time convincing me that it would support my weight. I had been fooled by solid-looking ice before. Finally they dragged me out onto the ice. At first I tested it nervously. Then slowly and hesitantly I began to trust the ice. We played all afternoon on the thick ice, and no one fell through. That fun afternoon is one of my fondest childhood memories.

My experiences with ice remind me of the philosophies and teachings in which we put our faith. We have to test them to make sure they're trustworthy. Many things that look good on the surface may, in fact, put us in peril. Perhaps you have skated on the thin ice of faith in the world and its enticing lies. And you fell through, with chilling consequences. Now you don't know if you can trust anything or anyone, let alone develop the faith that Hebrews 11:1 talks about: "Now faith is being sure of what we hope for and certain of what we do not see." As opposed to trusting in the things of the world, which you can at least experience with the senses, God asks you to trust in things that you can't even see.

It is understandable that you're reluctant to sign over your complete trust to what you are not certain of. But there is hope. First, the trust you offer God does not have to be that great to begin with. Jesus said that with just a mustard seed of faith you could see impossible and tremendous things happen in your life. Second, all you have to do is to take one little step onto the ice. Test it—God will not fail you. Soon, you will be running across the ice, taking some painful falls, but as you are racing to the other side, joy will eventually overtake you.

Perhaps you have been wounded by the world by believing in the glittering lies of sin. Perhaps you are tremendously discouraged, bitter, and resentful. Perhaps you are dealing with childhood memories of abuse or abandonment. Or maybe you feel lonely and isolated. Maybe you live, as I did, with the unwelcome company of your guilt and shame.

Whatever your situation, healing and growth will begin when you put your faith in God and, step by step, learn to place your full trust in Him. He will undergird you and support you, but the journey isn't always easy. By returning to God's narrow path, things might even get worse before they get better. But I want to emphasize that *things will get better.* If you truly have come to an end of yourself, this may be the only time when you can successfully return to the path that follows God. In a sense you are graced by your helplessness because He will surprise you with His grace, His love, and His plan for your life.

SEVEN

TRUE FAITH

Set Free to Follow the Narrow Path

D uring my junior and senior years in high school, I had a girlfriend named Sally. She was my first true love and everything any high school boy could want. She was a beautiful girl who had long blonde hair, an inviting smile, and a heart of laughter. Sally lived in a beautiful white house and had the best swimming pool in town. One summer, as she and her family were preparing to leave on vacation, her father asked me if I would take care of the pool, which looked something like the Romans would have constructed inside a fine palace. Always wanting to impress, I quickly agreed, considering it an honor somewhere up there with receiving the Purple Heart.

He took me to the pool and gave me instructions. He showed me how to test the water's pH level and how to take a sample of water and test it with chemicals from a pool kit. In a tube the sample would turn various shades of pink. The kit also included a tube with the standard; if my shade of pink matched this shade of pink, then it meant the pool was perfectly chlorinated. If it was too dark, the pool had too much chlorine; too pale, it had too little.

"No problem," I reassured him. "Just leave it to me."

During the first week, I was diligent in my duties. The pink was always perfect. I imagined myself both a scientist and a lifeguard as I lounged around the pool. The second week, however, I became a little lax about the whole affair. In fact I didn't even check on the pool until the day before Sally and her family were to come home. No problem, I reasoned. I had anticipated my absence by simply adding a bit more chlorine before I left. Clearly the family was lucky to have such a clever and resourceful person taking care of the pool.

I'll never forget walking up to the edge of the pool that day. The water looked like milk (no exaggeration)! The sparkling blue-green color was gone. I took out the testing kit and mixed the chemicals. The results showed my sample as far from the middle as possible. To say that I had dumped too much chlorine in the pool was to say that Chernobyl leaked a little radiation. Sally's father had shown me what to do if there was not enough chlorine, but I had no idea what to do with too much. I needed to act fast and clear out the milk—or else. The next stage, I imagined, would be cottage cheese. I didn't want the family to come home to a chunky-style pool.

I called a friend of mine whose father owned a pool chemical company. I begged and pleaded for help. Could he get his dad to come and take a look? Much to my relief, his father agreed to rush over and see if there was anything he might do; he probably understood the dire condition of the pool and me. When he arrived, he looked at the creamy pool, shook his head a few times, and went to his truck. Returning, he dumped a few bags of something in the water. He said it was potash. I wasn't sure what potash was—I guessed that marijuana smokers collected their ash and sold it to pool companies—but I was sure grateful that it existed. Within hours, the pool returned to its crystal green sparkling clarity.

When Sally and her family returned home, I was standing by the water, a regular pool magician. Her father smiled and thanked me. My girlfriend gave me a hug. The crisis had passed. Life was good again.

I mention this incident not so much to depict my irresponsibility but to share the lesson I learned over those weeks: if you deviate from the standard, the established guidelines, you will pay the consequences. As I stated before, anytime I journeyed off the narrow path in my life, I have had to learn that lesson again. Changing the standard doesn't alter our problems or remedy anything. If the shades of our actions deviate from the color of truth, we must change our actions, not try to alter the truth.

The Bible, the Word of God, is truth. It sets the ultimate standard. As such, the standard of truth is both impossibly bad and impossibly good news. It says that we are stained with sin, which sits dark and dismal in our hearts and minds. It says, too, that there is nothing we can do to make things right. But the good news is that though we cannot change our situation, there is One who can: God. Through the death and resurrection of Jesus Christ, our sins have been forgiven, death has been overcome, and a new life is possible for us.

Jesus said the truth would set us free. So why do so many of us feel so bound up, so tied to guilt, addiction, abuse, or lust? Do you ever wonder how other people find deep and vital faith? Do you ever wonder if there's a formula, some prescription of faith that will bring freedom?

When I first came to Christ, I longed for freedom—from the past, from worry, from the consequences of sin. Just the thought that I might have a chance of experiencing it gave me a glimmer of hope in the midst of an increasingly dim and damaged life. But soon I was leaving the path of truth for the broad road of bright illusion and tickling half-truths.

"The truth will set you free" has become a battle cry that dedicated Christians often use to attract others to the faith. But if the truth really sets people free, why are there so many Christians in bondage? If the truth sets people free, why do power-hungry preachers abuse their people with legalistic and binding views? If the truth sets people free, why are so many people in the church trapped in abusive relationships? If the truth sets people free, why do we see so many dedicated men and women of God fall victim to sexual temptation and destroy their ministries and marriages?

FOLLOW ME

Following Jesus means following the truth. Jesus made it clear: "I am the way and the truth and the life" (John 14:6). The way, the truth, and the life, then, are all connected in the person of Christ. You cannot follow Christ without following truth, and you cannot have life—abundant life on earth and eternal life in heaven—without a relationship with Christ.

This is where the narrow path becomes difficult. The truth, contrary to the voice of the world, is not relative and inclusive, bendable to fit our personal desires. The truth is permanent and inflexible, both the demanding rigidity of the law and the relentless love of grace. John F. Kennedy said, "The great enemy of the truth is very often not the lie—deliberate, contrived, and dishonest, but the myth—persistent, persuasive, and unrealistic." In our culture, two great and opposing myths prevail. One is the worship of self, which centers on the myth that there is a god inside each of us. The other extreme is the myth of fate, in which science tells us that we are controlled by our genes and our choices are determined by our inherited DNA codes. Both half-truths are twisted forms of the truth.

Although it is true that we were created to be "sons of God" (Rom. 8:14), we do not become so through our own effort. And although it is true that we are powerless to save ourselves, we are also free to obey and to live in the environment of grace (Rom. 6:17–18). In the myths described in the previous paragraph, the truth is twisted by impure motivation, founded on the need for power and control. One is blatant—I can do *anything,* and all I have to do is to try. The other is subtle—I can do *nothing,* so I won't even bother. In both cases the ultimate standard is the self. Such a demand for control, the Bible says, leads away from the truth. John 3:19 tells us, "This is the verdict: Light has come into the world, but men loved darkness instead of light because their deeds were evil." We would rather do anything (or nothing), it seems, than face up to the fullness of the facts.

The church is not immune to the influence of such powerful myths. Grace often seems anything but graceful. In His grace God often reveals the destructive power of our own sin. This is a painful process. Because we often see pain as something that should be avoided at all costs, we begin to believe that God doesn't really know what He is doing. We would rather look and feel better than *be* better. We don't understand the good news that God loves us and wants us to be conformed to the likeness of His Son. So we demand control, often settling for less than the truth.

Obedience involves *choosing* to give up control. Deciding to love God and others and overcome self-obsession is what makes the narrow path so narrow. Having faith in Christ alone is hard work. The glittering and easy lies of the world seem more appealing than God's hard (but wonderful) promises. Jesus didn't make an empty promise when He spoke about the power of truth, but He did place a few conditions on its setting us free: "If you hold to my teaching, you are really my disciples. Then you will know the truth, and the truth will set you free" (John 8:31–32).

God's truth will free us; the problem is that we seek our own comfort and control instead of seeking love. Although it may not be an overt act of rebellion against God, we may gradually drift away from the truth that could free us. Living according to Christ's teachings makes us unashamed disciples who daily discover a deeper and richer knowledge of the truth. That knowledge counters the wisdom of the world and allows us to walk freely in God's love and grace. It enables us to find fulfillment, meaning, and purpose. The price of freedom is the exchange of all the false teachings of the world and our self-constructed facades for a life of authentic Christianity.

We are to follow truth. And what path is that? Hebrews 12:2 points the way: "Let us fix our eyes on Jesus, the author and perfecter of our faith, who for the joy set before him endured the cross, scorning its shame, and sat down at the right hand of the throne of God."

Why are we so quick to believe what is false? Because we want to. We want to own, to possess, to hoard. And if we don't want actual power, we at least seek the power of certainty.

Enough of this living-by-faith stuff. When we reach such a point, though, we have lost faith in God's love. We can find that love again through the truths of the Bible. But it is up to us to make choices based on the truth and then follow through. As 2 Timothy 3:16–17 states, "All Scripture is God-breathed and is useful for teaching, rebuking, correcting and training in righteousness, so that the man of God may be thoroughly equipped for every good work."

Truth and love are inseparable twins. Both seek to give, to free, to offer hope. They never seek to set their own broad path. Rather, truth and love follow Jesus on the narrow and self-giving road.

GRACE TO BE HONEST

How can we remain faithful to truth if we are so predisposed to follow after soothing lies? First, we must believe the truth. We naturally tend to stray away from believing both the bad and the good news of the gospel. We forget about God's grace and become impressed with ourselves. We lose touch with the deadliness of sin. We forget to be honest.

James 5:16 is a verse often ignored in contemporary churches: "Confess your sins to each other and pray for each other so that you may be healed." When was the last time you heard someone confess his sins in a church setting? It doesn't happen very often because people are too afraid they will become the next topic of the gossip chain. People don't reveal their problems, so others don't know how to pray for them. As a result, they remain in their broken condition, attending church, but not really being part of the church. When the gospel's bad news—that we are all sinners—is no longer a dynamic reality, we miss out on the gospel's good news—that we are all forgiven.

Just because we receive grace does not mean that our struggles with sin are over. Just the opposite. God gives us grace so we can more fully know and confess our sins to one another. The Bible is brutally honest about its "saints." There were no angelic editors assigned to take out the "bad" parts, to tidy up the records of the biblical figures. If we think the royals in England have had problems with their marriages, they're nothing compared to the problems that David and his royal family had in the Bible. Adultery, murder, incest, and rape are all part of the biblical account of God's family. They are nothing new.

Even though problems are openly revealed throughout Scripture, the church has somehow gotten the notion that hiding is more important than healing. We put on happy faces and act as if everything is wonderful. We fake it, then get into the car and go back home. We complain that we aren't getting what we need from church, and we criticize the staff for not doing a better job. Rather than change, we continue to live behind masks and play out our roles, trapped inside the illusions we have created to keep people from knowing who we really are.

We must understand and believe that through repentance,

grace removes sin, leaving us free and transformed. The myths of the world—that we are basically good or completely fated—disappear in the truth of God's grace.

A few years ago, I met with a suicidal woman at the request of her pastor. When she arrived at my office, she was one of the most distressed-looking people I had ever seen. I had been told she was a model at one time, but I couldn't see any evidence of it. My assistant took care of her three-year-old child while I attempted to provide some hope. The woman was full of venom and bitterness. I had never heard anyone more capable of spewing foul words. In between her expletives I tried to get her to consider the issue of forgiveness—that she needed to forgive others and allow God to forgive her.

This woman was convinced that God had turned His back on her. Nothing I said made any difference. She responded to me as if I were a piece of wood. My attempts to communicate hope or a way out of her mess were futile. As she got up to leave, I made one last-ditch effort to help her. I reached over and took the wrapping off a new Life Recovery Bible and handed it to her. I told her that God's Word is far more powerful than anything I could say, and I encouraged her to take the Bible and read it. At that point I could not imagine the slightest possibility that she would follow through. Watching her walk out the door, I was convinced that I would get a call within the week telling me she had taken her life.

Two months later, I was invited to preach at the church she attended. Just before the service, I saw a very attractive woman clutching a ragged-looking Life Recovery Bible. The suicidal woman had undergone an obvious and dramatic transformation. She had a smile on her face and a glint in her eyes.

When she approached me, I asked what she had done with herself. She looked at me and said, "I stopped believing the lies of Satan and started believing the truth of Jesus Christ."

She went on to say that she had spent a lot of time reading God's Word and going to church to learn more about the truth. It was one of the most joyous and fulfilling events of my life—a great surprise by God. By believing and living according to the truth, this woman was able to find hope in the midst of overwhelming problems.

If you are experiencing misery, despair, and hopelessness, perhaps you have become confused about the truth. Perhaps you have bought into some of the myths of this world. If you are willing to live by the truth, it will transform your life by giving you hope and confidence. Permanent, rock-solid, and never-changing, truth has the power to turn lives around.

The Soldier of Truth

What if we really believed the promises of God were true? What if we lived in faith that He would provide rest, shelter, food, love, forgiveness, and abundant life? Would we not be ready to bet our very lives on His words? Would we not be willing to take risks to love others and God more fully, with less anxiety and fear?

Of course we would. But in a fallen world, truth is never easy to follow, no matter how much faith we have. And as we've discussed, truth is not always something we care to hear. Jesus told His disciples that one of them would betray Him, and sure enough, Judas proved that Christ was a man of His word. Peter also proved the truth of Christ's words when he denied his Lord. Jesus tells us similar truths about our lives that we would rather not hear. He also tells us that, in a world bent on self-destruction, the truth will be despised. As fallen creatures, we forget that there is a Source of absolute truth, and if we hold on to Him, we will find fulfillment and freedom.

All of us need to examine our lives and uncover the half-truths, myths, and encumbrances that stand in the way of our relationship with God. Is it money? Is it lust? Is it alcohol? Is it power? It's important to be aware of the sin that hinders us from achieving Christ's call on our lives. To me, one of the most frightening scriptures speaks of people who believe they are serving God but really aren't. Christ tells us that when He returns, some people who claim to have been serving Him will say, "I have done great things in Your name, Lord. I have healed people. I have prophesied." Christ will say to them, "I never knew you" (Matt. 7:22–23). They thought they had it. But in the hot light of God's truth, their false idols melt.

EIGHT

DENY THE WORLD

Learning to Hold Things Loosely

I looked up at the hills surrounding my town and watched, along with my coworkers, the firestorm rip through the beautiful hills of Laguna Beach. The fire had already destroyed more than two hundred homes on the north side of the town. We watched in total silence—fearful and awed at the sight.

On an otherwise beautiful morning in October 1993, I left the office early. My home of ten years was in the path of the fire. On my drive home I confessed to the Lord about my struggle with materialism. I prayed some dangerous prayers:

Lord, help me to release my grip on things. Later that day as I began to load belongings into two cars and my friend Burt Wilson's Toyota pickup, I could see the fire slowly creep toward my street. With such little space and time, I faced critical decisions about what we considered valuable.

I was surprised how little there was that I really cared about. God had obviously been working in my life. The first thing I loaded into the trunk of my car was my collection of ukuleles. Having fought against depression a good deal of my life, I had learned a valuable lesson: it is almost impossible to be depressed while playing a ukulele. Next, I packed photos and video-tapes—priceless and irreplaceable snapshots of what I thought was a dream.

Ukuleles, snapshots, videos, and my two-and-a-half-year-old Madeline. What else really mattered?

I climbed onto the roof of my house and doused it with water even though I knew it probably wouldn't do any good. I could see some of the other houses on our street already starting to burn. There were no fire trucks—not even the sound of a far-off siren—because they had all been dispatched to other locations. Only the hungry sound of fire broke the silence. There was clearly no hope of saving our home.

Madeline rode down in one of the cars, and we all agreed to meet at the McDonald's in Dana Point, just a short distance away. As I desperately watered my roof, the police arrived, their bullhorns blaring.

"The fires are burning on this street!" the officers announced.

"You must abandon your homes and leave, or you might not be able to."

The whole town was being evacuated. I could see a huge tanker aircraft flying overhead, dropping fire retardant. I climbed down from the roof and decided to make a final search of the house. Had we forgotten anything of value? I ran, looking through each room, but didn't find anything. While rushing for the front door, I saw out of the corner of my eye a small shiny green vinyl froggy purse—Madeline's prized possession. It cost maybe $2.50. Acting on impulse, I tucked the purse under my arm and locked the front door. Climbing into my car, I tossed the purse into the backseat.

I drove away from our house, overwhelmed with grief. Even though my search hadn't revealed anything else worth taking, it was still painful to think of all our worldly possessions going up in smoke, not to mention our beloved house. We would be stripped of something dear to us. Sure, it was just wood, vinyl, and glass, but it had been our home for a decade.

When I arrived at McDonald's, I found my family. We all were very upset because we thought our house was gone. We agreed to spend the night in Newport Beach, and I decided Madeline would ride with me. I strapped her into the seat beside me. (Car seats were not a requirement back then.)

While we were driving, she looked up at me and asked in her little-girl way, "Daddy, house burned down?"

"Madeline, we don't know if it burned down. We won't know for a couple of days."

All at once, a horrible, sad look appeared on Madeline's face. "Daddy," she said. "FORGOT MY FROGGY PURSE!"

With one eye on the road, I reached around into the backseat. My hand found that green cheap piece of shiny vinyl. I handed it to her—and I became an instant hero.

A huge grin covered her face as she hugged my right arm and said, "Thank you, Daddy."

At that moment I wouldn't have taken $20,000 for that ridiculous purse.

Fortunately for us, Madeline's purse wasn't the only thing that survived our near tragedy. Our entire house was spared. Just after I had left our house, the fire department decided that if they didn't stop the fire at our street, the houses down the hill would burn because most of them had wooden roofs. And if that happened, the fire would have continued to burn out of control, putting the whole town in jeopardy. The firemen made a daring and courageous stand. Just ten houses away from ours, they stopped the progress of the fire.

In the shadow of that awful blaze, God taught me an invaluable lesson: the kingdom principle of what's really valuable. So close to having all of my belongings consumed by a raging inferno, I discovered that there are very few things I can't live without. Of course it would have been difficult, perhaps even devastating, to lose our home and its contents. But through that I learned they're just things, and they matter very little in the grand scheme of life. I had discovered how to hold things loosely. Doing that, I discovered freedom.

NINE

DENY YOURSELF

*Giving Ourselves Away for
the Sake of Others*

Afew years back, I went on a business trip to Fairbanks, Alaska. I went in January—not the best time to visit Alaska. During the winter in Fairbanks, the sun never comes up, and the cold is deeper and more penetrating than you can imagine. After landing at the airport, which was covered with a light-blue permafrost, I walked off the airplane and into 40-below temperature. I could barely breathe. Before I could take my rental car, the attendant had to unplug the engine heater (used to keep the fluids from freezing).

Checking into my hotel, I made my way to the restaurant

to grab a bite to eat. While I was eating, a man came in and sat down at the table next to me. His cologne arrived a couple of seconds before he did. But that's not all he exuded. He had the air of a rich man about him. For some reason I remember exactly how this man looked, right down to the finest detail: a navy blazer with bright gold buttons; the kind of Italian loafers that wealthy people wear, which make their feet look a couple of sizes smaller; a flashy gold watch; perfectly coifed hair; a steady, firm gaze.

As I eyed this man, he occasionally glanced my way, and I acted as if I hadn't seen him. In my mind I was judging him, dismissing him as an arrogant, pompous man. *Oh, brother*, I snickered to myself. *Look at this guy. He really thinks he's something.*

Slyly watching the man, I noticed him call the wine steward to his table. Not surprisingly he ordered a bottle of the best red wine in the house. The wine steward was obviously excited, working hard to display whatever charm he possessed. I imagined he was thinking, *Big tip!* After the steward uncorked the bottle, the man took it and inhaled the aroma. I wondered how he could smell anything over his powerful cologne. Next, the steward poured some wine into what looked like a baby rattle that hung from his neck. He was tasting the wine for the man, as if he were the cupbearer for King Nebuchadnezzar and there was risk that some conspirator might poison him. The steward then poured a little into a glass for the man, who swirled it around and sniffed the wine. Then he threw his head back and rolled it around in his mouth. He looked as if he was about to gargle. I thought, *If he doesn't like it, he's going to spit it out all over me and everyone around him.* I scooted over a bit just in case.

It was fascinating. This man was totally immersed in the ritual. It must have been good wine, for with a nod of his head to the steward, his glass was filled. Next, he made a motion with his arm, and the steward leaned over as the rich man whispered something in his ear. Unexpectedly the steward picked up the wine bottle, put it on his tray, and set out across the dining room.

I looked around and saw several attractive women on the other side of the room. *Great,* I thought. *In addition to this guy smelling like the cologne counter at Saks Fifth Avenue, now he's acting like a shark smelling a kill.* He could probably harpoon any woman's heart with his money and charm. I was starting to lose my appetite.

Beyond the good-looking women, I noticed an elderly woman sitting by herself in the corner. She was overweight, and her face was leathery. She had matted hair and wore a tattered old coat with an ugly scarf. I wondered how she could let herself be seen like that in a public place.

As I returned my gaze to the steward, I watched him walk past one beautiful woman and then another. My eyes stayed one step ahead of him, trying to guess which attractive woman would be the lucky one tonight. Which of these ladies would be the one recipient of this man's gift? Much to my surprise, the steward stopped at the table of the elderly disheveled woman.

He whispered something in her ear, which seemed to embarrass her. Then he poured her a glass of wine. With that, he stepped back. The woman held up her glass and looked over at the rich man, who raised his glass in return. Across the room, they shared a toast from the best bottle of wine in the house.

I have often thought about that moment—not only about my critical, judgmental attitude toward both the rich man and the elderly woman, but also about the scene as a metaphor of grace. Who could imagine such a gift on that cold, dark night in the deep Alaskan winter? This rich man could have chosen any number of beautiful women to charm and entice, but instead he lavished an expensive gift on a wrinkled woman dressed in rags. What would possess him to do such a thing? What a surprising, unselfish act!

The man's generosity reminded me of God's grace toward each of us. He owns the cattle on a thousand hills. He created the cosmos, He arranged the millions of planets that sparkle in the sky, and He has the power to control every atom and molecule. And yet He gives us every good and perfect gift. He could have chosen only the beautiful people, the put-together people to receive His blessings. But instead He says, "I have chosen the lowly, the foolish, the weak, and the despised people of the world" (see 1 Cor. 1:27–29). While we were still sinners, Christ died for us, shedding His blood, the wine of the new covenant.

But that was only the beginning of God's gifts to us. Here is just a partial list of His surprises:

- "New birth into a living hope through the resurrection of Jesus Christ from the dead" (1 Peter 1:3).

- "His glorious grace, which he has freely given us in the One he loves" (Eph. 1:6).

- Salvation and the call to a holy life—"not because of anything we have done but because of his own purpose and grace" (2 Tim. 1:9).

- "Different gifts, according to the grace given us" (Rom. 12:6).

- "Everything we need for life and godliness through our knowledge of him who called us by his own glory and goodness" (2 Peter 1:3).

- All of His "great and precious promises, so that through them [we] may participate in the divine nature and escape the corruption in the world caused by evil desires" (2 Peter 1:4).

- "The Spirit as a deposit, guaranteeing what is to come"—righteousness, eternal life, heaven, and adoption as children of God (2 Cor. 5:5).

TEN

GIVING AND SERVING

Investing in Things That Really Matter

A few years ago, I was invited to a special wedding. The father of the bride, Hal Asher, was a dear and treasured friend. When the invitation arrived, we wanted to purchase the most expensive wedding gift we had ever bought, and that is exactly what we did—as much to show respect for Hal as to help the young couple.

I had met Hal when his advertising agency handled the account for a company where I had worked. For some reason he liked me and helped me survive the first difficult years of my marriage. When we were really struggling, Hal gave us an all-expense-paid vacation to the Caribbean. No one had ever done anything like that for us, and no one has done anything similar since. Hal always went out of his way to encourage us.

Hal was a successful and busy man. He had dined with many stars who had worked with him on commercials, and he knew how to entertain people royally. When he heard that my parents were coming to town for a visit, he insisted on taking them out to dinner at a restaurant near his Beverly Hills home. For my parents, who lived in rural Texas, a Beverly Hills dinner with the head of an advertising agency was a once-in-a-lifetime experience. After arriving at Hal's home, where we ate enough hors d'oeuvres to constitute an entire meal, we were off to the Palm restaurant for a dinner that my parents never forgot. Hal ordered for all of us since he had been there many times. When the food arrived, my folks could not believe their eyes. Set before them were two huge lobsters, weighing about twenty pounds each. One claw on those lobsters was bigger than any whole lobster I have ever eaten. My dad ate and ate and smiled and laughed and ate and told his corny jokes and ate more until he had devoured the entire lobster.

For the rest of my father's life, he continued to talk about that evening. As a storyteller, he probably got more mileage out of that one evening than any other single event in his life. Needless to say, I am forever indebted to Hal Asher for giving my father one of the greatest evenings of his life, not to mention all the other things he did for me.

So when I learned that this dear man's daughter was getting

married, I wanted to honor him, and I could not do that by scrimping on a gift. I spent more money than I had, but the sacrifice was worth it. He recognized that I had done something special—not so much to benefit the bride, whom I hardly knew, but to show my appreciation to him.

From the wedding I learned a valuable lesson that applies to my spiritual life: you can't throw pennies at the bride and expect the father to be honored. Mediocre, perfunctory, or hand-me-down gifts won't get the job down. For a gift to be of real value, given from the heart, only a gift that requires sacrifice will do.

GENEROUS GIFTS FOR THE BRIDE

The New Testament frequently refers to the church as the bride of Christ. As members of the church, we have been given precious, valuable gifts that God desires us to use sacrificially for the bride of Christ. But don't we often give to the bride only what is convenient? We look for flashy, big, and expensive-looking things, or we dig through our spiritual cedar chests for a token we can toss at the bride's feet. When we offer only casual and convenient gifts to the church, Christ's bride, how do you think that makes the Father feel?

The wedding of Hal Asher's daughter caused me to rethink my view of the church. The church is more than just another organization committed to good and moral causes. It's a living, divine organism, which demands us to give not only our gifts but also our very selves.

When Jesus asked Peter if he loved Him, Peter replied three times that, of course, he did. And after each response, Jesus told Peter to "feed My sheep." Jesus meant that as proof of his love, Peter should care for and nurture His church, His precious and lovely bride. Jesus did not tell Peter to start something big or build a spectacular building. He didn't tell him to use his organizational skills to start a massive movement. His instructions for showing love were simple: take care of My bride. The same standard applies to all of us. Are we giving gifts—our money, time, or energy—to the church as an act of love for God?

We judge churches by many standards—the number of members, the number of ministries, the quality of outreach programs, the pastor's reputation, and so on. But the one true standard of the church should be this: Are its people giving sacrificially and serving others out of love for God? Even though it is faith that saves us, it is service to others that fulfills us.

My father would not have been considered a wealthy man by many standards, but he was one of the richest men I have known. His life was a model of service to the church and other people. One of my earliest memories of my father was his taking our family to the "wrong side of the tracks" to help needy people. We would carry food to those who lived in one-room houses, many of which had no source of heat. We didn't have much money, but we still gave to those who had less. My father taught me many valuable lessons in servanthood.

Near the end of his life, he was still serving. After my brother Jerry died of AIDS, my father (and my mother) visited prisons and hospitals where people were dying of AIDS. In those places he would share God's love and the good news of the gospel. My father could have easily lost himself in the pain of his son's homosexuality; he could have turned away from those who had the same disease that took one of his boys. But my father was wiser and richer than that. He knew that life, real and true life, comes in service to others.

My dad died a few years ago, at the age of sixty-eight, from a massive heart attack. At his funeral the pastor mentioned the balance between faith and works.

"When it came to the life of Walter Arterburn," he said, "there was never any question or doubt about whether faith or works were more important. In his life he had incredible faith, and he put it to work serving people."

My father rarely lost sight of what was real. It wasn't the stuff of the world—what you could touch, feel, hear, smell, and see—that was important and real, but what was invisible, the unseen qualities of love, faith, grace, and hope. He knew that giving of himself—his kindness, service, and his money—was what really mattered. By giving he received much in return.

When It's Difficult to Serve

The narrow path that Jesus prescribed for us is traveled very slowly, on our knees in service to others. Many people in the church, however, find this difficult to do. Sometimes people erroneously believe that serving others is an "answer" to their own hardships. They serve dutifully and religiously so that God will bless them and take their problems away. They seek to please others to appear pleasing. These people often "abandon" their own needs and problems to serve others. But because they don't understand that their own needs and desires still control their motivation, they become disappointed and bitter in their service.

The call to serve others doesn't paint a picture of men and women drained and empty, devoid of energy and enthusiasm. God's call to serve the church doesn't mean we should deny our legitimate human needs or all of the desires and passions that He has placed within us. Jesus took care of Himself physically and emotionally, and He challenged His followers to embrace their uniqueness and pursue the dreams God had given them. But just as Jesus did, we must allow God to determine which needs are legitimate. We must yield our desires and passions to His guidance and invest our energies in ways that build His kingdom.

Some people are self-absorbed, lost in their problems and needs. "I can't serve others," they honestly admit, "because I am too messed up." They never seek understanding of the deeper spiritual and emotional issues that fuel their root problems. Consequently they remain trapped in their pain. No matter how bad the cards that have been dealt to you, you can learn to give of yourself in service to God. Your pain can be powerfully transformed into purpose.

That is the beauty of God's plan, the full circle of His redemptive love. Those in need are lovingly served and are slowly and gradually transformed by such love. Then they, too, can begin to serve others in need. And the cycle—once a destructive path of pain—becomes infused with the healing powers of God.

GIVING BACK TO GOD WHAT BELONGS TO HIM

God is a Gift Giver who desires for us to use those gifts to serve Him. His plan is as natural as a river flowing into a sea. That is the simple beauty of God's design. But because we live in a country with so many things and so many opportunities, we may lose sight of the reality that every gift is from God. We forget that everything belongs to God and we are simply stewards of what we've been given. Our materialistic, image-obsessed culture often keeps us from seeing things as we should.

As I mentioned earlier, before I was married, I went on a mission trip to India. The country is so poor that begging has been organized into networks called begging rings. People in these organizations often maim and disable their own children so they will appear more pathetic, generating more sympathy and, they hope, more money. Then disabled people grow up and find little else they can do to earn a living.

Many of these beggars congregate outside the city in slums. I'll never forget the church service we attended in one of those slums, named Koramangala, which was little more than a collection of shacks made of wood scraps and cardboard. As we prepared for the service, we watched those poor people hobble up the street where open sewage was flowing around them. Slowly and carefully they made their way to the front of the shack that served as a church and gave their money as an offering.

Those people—disabled, impoverished, and rejected by the world—truly believed that everything they had was God's. To honor God, they wanted to give a portion (if not all) back to Him. They had pure motivations for giving to God. They didn't give to get, they gave out of deep conviction that all gifts should return to the Giver.

Giving sacrificially to God cannot be just a compartment of our lives, like watching football on Sunday afternoon or preparing a budget. It should be the overriding passion of who we are. We should return everything we have—our money, time, energy, talents, hearts, and minds—to Him in love through serving others. This is not always easy, pleasant, or glamorous. We will probably never win an award or be featured on TV because of our service. A good deal of the service we do for others will be tedious and uninspiring.

The book of Revelation says that there will be a great wedding feast between Jesus Christ and His bride, the church. Revelation 19:9 states, "Blessed are those who are invited to the wedding supper of the Lamb!" In my mind I picture a huge reception hall, with golden tables and a twelve-story cake studded with emeralds and sapphires. After the angels stop singing their wedding songs, the crowd will separate to allow Jesus to pass through to a table in the center of the room. On it are the gifts to the bride. Which ones will be yours?

ELEVEN

THE PLACE OF PAIN

How Suffering Refines Our Faith

I have written and spoken about my twenty-year marriage coming to an end after I discovered my wife's unfaithfulness with someone whom I had thought was a good friend. Within days of me confronting her, she filed for divorce, and the marriage was over. It was the end of twenty years of toil and struggle. It had been that way from the beginning.

At first each of us assumed that we had married the wrong person. Little seemed right about our relationship, and each day brought with it some new difficulty or conflict. Of course, each of us thought the other was completely at fault. We looked as if we had our act together, but behind the facade we were hiding a deep, painful secret about our relationship, one that we rarely talked about even with each other.

Ironically we had joined a support group of four couples at church. The theory was that we would share our problems and help one another. Our group included a pastor and his wife, a baseball player and his wife, a government official and his wife, a psychologist and his wife, and us. What was designed to facilitate authenticity became a sorry example of how people with big needs can hide them, even while meeting with each other face-to-face.

Week after week we went to this superficial group. Each couple shared only those things that were safe. It was like an adult game of hide-and-seek. All of us needed each other; in fact two other couples had marriages that were in big trouble, too, but no one would risk the vulnerability required to be open, honest, and authentic.

One night as we were coming home, we agreed that if we were going to belong to this group and spend this much time with them, we were going to share what was really going on in our lives. So the next week we went back to the group committed to telling the truth.

When the sharing started, we broke in and said, "It's time that we reveal what we're really dealing with. We've been married a year, and the sexual intimacy part of our marriage isn't working. You can count on one hand the number of times we've even tried to be intimate with each other. Both of us looked forward to this part of marriage, but it just hasn't happened."

I will never forget the looks on the faces of those people. It was as if we had dumped a truckload of radioactive material into the living room. There was a lot of shifting in seats, coughing, and looking at the floor. They just didn't know what to do. Instead of creating an opportunity for all of us to be genuine, our honesty came as a threat. I think each member of the group instinctively knew that since we had revealed our pain and struggle, we had earned the right to confront them about the true nature of their relationships. That was the last time the group ever met. No one came back, and we were left feeling embarrassed and humiliated.

HIDING BEHIND FACADES

Why do Christians, who are supposed to be committed to the truth, often seem to be the most fake people on earth? One reason is that we've been told—either outright or subtly—that Christians shouldn't struggle. The message is, if only we had enough faith, our conflicts and problems would resolve themselves. If we're good Christians, we'll have it all together. So we hide our struggles behind polished masks.

Many people expect that God will give them lives of ease and comfort once they accept Christ. This Sunday, from hundreds of church pulpits, a message will be preached: "If you will come to Christ, your problems will disappear because Christ is the answer. You will have a Christian home, and if you pray for your children, then they will grow up to be wonderful Christians, too, protected by the hand of God."

The problem is in how people twist the meaning of Christ's promise of joy. They believe it to mean living near perfect lives, free from struggle and pain. A slick advertisement put together by the Mormon Church portrayed a perfect couple, with perfect white teeth, holding a perfect child. They were rowing across a perfect little lake on a perfect evening when the sun spread a perfect rose color across the water. The message, of course, was this: become a Mormon and you, too, will have a perfect life. That may make a good ad, but it sure won't translate into real life.

The same is true with the Christian faith. If you expect the Christian walk to be a stroll through the park, think again. Becoming a Christian does not remove struggle from your life; in fact it often *adds* to the struggle or intensifies it. Some of the most committed Christians have lived some of the most difficult lives.

The great theologian Dietrich Bonhoeffer said, "When Christ calls a person, he bids that person to come and die." Jesus never promised you a rose garden. When He stood with His frightened disciples after His resurrection, He showed them the scars on His hands and side. Then He told them, "As the Father has sent Me, I am sending you" (John 20:21). The path that Jesus wants us to follow leads through the pain of the Cross; He tells us to pick up our crosses and follow Him (Luke 9:23).

As Christians, we don't have the option of running from pain and struggle. Pain is as much a part of this world as are beauty and free will. To pretend otherwise is to dismiss reality. Some people will go to unbelievable extremes to avoid pain. Unfortunately this is true of many Christians. Like the people in the small group I described earlier, Christians hide behind facades, jargon, niceties, and rules. They lose themselves in the false hope that one day everything will be perfect. But because they are not dealing with the realities of life, they soon find themselves self-absorbed, without love for others or for God.

When we face the fact that the world is a messy place—that love is often tinged with betrayal, that children sometimes die of cancer, that dreams often end up shattered—we can learn from that pain that we are helpless without God. And depending on God is the healthy outcome of pain.

AUTHENTIC CHRISTIANITY

What does it mean to have an authentic Christian faith? What does it require? Some Christians act as though they have achieved a level of faith that places them above the tough realities of life. They lead us to believe they are "first-class" Christians who have found the secret to a near perfect life, devoid of pain. This concept is not only wrong; it is toxic.

The authentic Christian life doesn't involve attaining perfection, and it doesn't mean living free from struggle; instead, it deals head-on with the issue of pain. Rather than trying to avoid pain, as authentic Christians we allow struggle to shape our hearts and our faith. We allow humility to draw us farther out of ourselves and closer to God. It is not an easy life, but it is a rich life, full of growth and tough moments that remind us of who we are and how far we have to go in our spiritual journey. In the face of pain and struggle, our faith will give us comfort, guidance, and hope.

The biblical view of life is that it often gets worse before it gets better. Salvation, the free gift of God, is sometimes painful. Listen to the apostle Peter address the value of suffering:

> Now for a little while you may have had to suffer grief in all kinds of trials. These have come so that your faith—of greater worth than gold, which perishes even though refined by fire—may be proved genuine and may result in praise, glory and honor when Jesus Christ is revealed. Though you have not seen him, you love him; and even though you do not see him now, you believe in him and are filled with an inexpressible and glorious joy, for you are receiving the goal of your faith, the salvation of your souls. (1 Peter 1:6–9)

In Romans Paul also described this refining process of suffering: "We also rejoice in our sufferings, because we know that suffering produces perseverance; perseverance, character; and character, hope. And hope does not disappoint us, because God has poured out his love into our hearts by the Holy Spirit, whom he has given us" (5:3–5). This, of course, does not mean we should act happy when we find out a leg has to be amputated or we have a terminal illness.

It does mean that one day we will rejoice at the adversities we faced and the way Christ brought us through them.

In my life suffering has taught me some of the deepest lessons of faith. For seven years I waited for a child. I prayed and begged God, but nothing happened. For seven long years we did everything that the infertility doctors suggested, but nothing worked. With each passing month our despair grew as we realized we could never have children.

Finally, through circumstances only God could have arranged, we were able to adopt our daughter, Madeline. She has become the light of our lives. This child is even more precious to us because we know she is a direct gift from God. Nothing we could have done would have brought Madeline to us.

Although the suffering seemed unbearable at times, the ordeal taught lessons that could not have been learned otherwise. Pain can be a powerful teacher because it forces us to understand that change and struggle are necessary to the maturation process.

CAN YOU SPARE SOME CHANGE?

My parents were godly Christians. Yet suffering brought them face-to-face with change that they never anticipated. Learning that their son was dying of AIDS forced them to see the difficult realities of life. Like many other Christians, they thought that if they honored God and dedicated their children to the Lord, we would be shielded from pain and suffering. They discovered, the hard way, that this belief was false.

God had allowed Jerry to contract AIDS after becoming

involved in the homosexual lifestyle. My parents wrestled not only with losing Jerry but also with feeling guilt: What could they have done differently to keep their son from such deadly behavior? Their faith did not protect them from falling apart in a mixture of sorrow and regret.

God used that terrible incident to mold and deepen their faith. When Jerry needed them most, my parents were able to display the courage and forgiveness necessary to lead him to repentance. They also developed deep compassion for others as a result of their suffering. Their hearts and lives were forever changed.

Change is always difficult, no matter what the situation entails. Most of us love the status quo. We grow comfortable and choose to ignore aspects of our lives that need improvement. But sometimes God asks us to make adjustments in areas we would rather just leave alone. Sometimes He asks us to change a career; other times it's a change in our perspective about money or priorities.

Change is never easy, especially after years of living a certain way. Responding to God's call to change can be painful because it often requires a transformation beyond what we thought possible. Nevertheless, what is impossible for us to achieve alone is possible through the power of God.

THE END OF SELF

Sometimes our lives seem to get worse because God wants to show us that He is our only hope. If we can control something on our own, we will never come to know the greater power of

God. God loves to step in and prove His faithfulness to us. No matter what the circumstances, God is still in control and will act according to His eternal plan. Isaiah 30:18 tells us the Lord is a God of justice for those who wait on Him. He will not abandon us in our times of helplessness. We must trust that He is able to change the worst situation into a time of hope and joy.

Donna lived with her husband and two babies on the tiny pension he received from the navy. Their rent was more than half of their income. Needless to say, the money often ran out. One month, their financial situation was so bad that Donna literally had no money left to buy laundry soap to wash her babies' dirty diapers.

Donna got on her knees in the kitchen and prayed, "God, I've never needed You like I need You now. I have nothing, and I need You to provide soap to wash these diapers."

Hearing a noise at the front door, Donna got up and went to open it. Someone had left a sample of soap in a plastic bag on her doorstep. It was a promotional giveaway. But Donna knew better. In utter helplessness she had cried out to God for help. Some would call the provision a coincidence, but Donna knew it was an act of God.

God wants you to see Him as your only real hope. Through the pain, God will act to show you that He cares for you personally and deeply. Rather than give up on Him, you must surrender faith in yourself so you can tap into God's divine power.

GOD OF THE IMPOSSIBLE

When things appear to be most impossible, God can show us He is in control. Our trials can become landmarks on our spiritual journey. We learn from Mark 10:27: "With man [it] is impossible, but not with God; all things are possible with God." Countless people in the Bible faced "impossible" situations, only to be delivered by a loving God. Gideon's armies, greatly outnumbered, defeated their enemies. The Israelites, pinned against the Red Sea by a fierce Egyptian army, crossed to safety on dry land. Paul, imprisoned in a dark cell, was able to sing songs of praise. In our troubles we must find the courage to believe that nothing is impossible with God.

One of my favorite verses in the Bible is John 11:39, which I like to paraphrase, "He stinketh." If there is something in your life that stinks, just remember that Lazarus, four days dead, also reeked to high heaven. Even when all hope was gone, Jesus showed His remarkable power and love by resurrecting Lazarus. If He can do that, He can give you new life and hope.

SHARING THE SUFFERINGS OF CHRIST

There is still another reason God allows us to endure heartache. Sometimes He permits our lives to deteriorate into a dark chasm of pain because He wants us to share in the sufferings of Jesus Christ. As the apostle Paul said, "I want to know Christ and the power of his resurrection and the fellowship of sharing in his sufferings" (Phil. 3:10). This last reason is perhaps the most painful, but it also produces the greatest spiritual growth and understanding of God's nature.

If in some small way we can begin to understand the depths of suffering that Christ endured for us, then we will draw even closer to Him. In these agonizing times we are invited to meet Jesus as a suffering Savior who willingly endured extreme hardship, even the pain of crucifixion, because He loved us so much. We can understand this suffering love only if we share in the suffering with Him.

There have been painful times in my life when I have had nothing to hold me up but the knowledge that Christ had suffered before me and was suffering with me. These experiences have taught me new dimensions of Christ's suffering love.

On April 1, 1995, my five-year-old daughter and I set off for our first rides on brand-new bicycles. Just past our house is a fork in the road: one way leads up a steep hill; the other way leads down an equally steep slope. Madeline and I approached the fork and were preparing to go up. Riding behind Madeline, I glanced down at my bike chain for just a moment. When I looked back up, I was horrified to see that she was beginning to roll *down* the hill.

She was picking up speed and heading for either a large metal Dumpster in front of a house under construction or a six-foot drop-off onto a concrete slab. Neither option would have had a very pretty outcome. Judging by her speed, I envisioned her receiving a smashed-up face and broken bones—or worse. I watched in horror as she tried to figure out how to make the brakes work. Unfortunately one pedal was up and one was down, and she didn't realize that she had to pedal forward before she could be in a position to brake. My precious little girl was on a runaway bicycle!

I knew I had to respond quickly. Jumping off my bicycle, I sprinted after her. I was wearing a T-shirt, a pair of shorts, and some loafers. I ran faster than I have ever run in my life. I ran so fast that I slipped out of my shoes. I ran so hard that the pavement severely bruised bones in my heels and soles, which took months to heal. I ran so swiftly that I seemed to be moving with supernatural speed.

When I caught up with my daughter seconds before she hit the Dumpster, I was able to lunge and grab her by the back of her sweater, veering her away from the huge metal monster. But we weren't out of danger. She and I and the bicycle crashed together and slid on the rough pavement. Fortunately I somehow managed to get between her and the street.

After we came to a stop, Madeline untangled herself from the heap of metal, rubber, skin, and bones. As she stood up, I looked her over. She was perfectly intact, without a scratch. She looked at me and immediately began to cry when she saw that I was covered with blood. In her mind I had just made it into the Owie Hall of Fame.

I had never experienced that kind of pain and blood loss. There were places on my feet that were scraped to the bone, which required a tetanus shot and antibiotics. I had taken a handlebar to my ribs and had pedal marks across my lower back. Twenty-three places on my feet, legs, knees, arms, and back were scraped, cut, and bruised from the pavement.

Slowly standing up to assess the damage to my body, I almost couldn't breathe. I looked at Madeline again and then back down at my wounds, but rather than join her in her tears, a huge grin spread over my face. Seeing Madeline in such good shape, I realized I had sacrificed my body for someone I love. For the first time I had saved someone I love dearly from pain. I was ecstatic in suffering love.

The experience gave me a new realization of Christ's love for me. I understand that His motive and willingness to die for me on the cross sprang from pure and undying love. That painful bicycle wreck made me more secure in my faith. I felt a fellowship with the Savior that I would not have known otherwise.

I don't know of anyone who gets excited about the possibility of his life becoming more painful and difficult. We all want to stay on the easy path. Biblical history and even our own lives show that more often than not, when we accept God's truth, we are in for a tough journey that will require a deep faith if we are to endure.

Yes, when we respond to God, things often get worse before they get better. But God has promised that if we have trust in Him, He will turn our suffering into joy—and refine our faith in the process. With endurance our lives and faith become deeper and richer.

TWELVE

CHRIST'S WOUNDS

The Consequences of His Grace

Recently I spoke at a church near Newark, New Jersey, on the concept of reproducing our sins in our children. A man came up to me afterward, deeply troubled. When he heard that the sins of the father could be passed on to the children, he was racked with guilt and fear because his past was so full of wrongdoing and rebellion. His father had been quite a sinner, and many of the things this man had done were repetitions of his father's rebellion.

As I talked to him, though, I found one critical difference between his father and himself—he was remorseful about his sin, and his father never had been. I told him that because of his repentant heart, he had an opportunity to be part of a transitional generation in his family. That is, he could be the one to break the chain of sin that had been passed down from generation to generation. He could accept Christ's free gift of healing and pass it on to his children.

When we parted ways a few minutes later, this man left with renewed hope. He realized that his life was far from doomed. By God's grace he was becoming a new man, a new creature, and he could set a godly example for his children.

Jesus Christ, the Great Healer, acts to set things right. In faith we must allow His power to work within us to heal our wounds; if we don't, we are likely to ignore them or, worse, attempt to heal ourselves. And sometimes in our pain we will venture back onto the broad path to find a quick and easy balm. Doing this creates still more wounds, though.

Instead of letting our pain drive us into more sin, we should let it drive us to God. To repentance. To the hope of healing and new life. Once we honestly face the reality of our wounds, God honors our faith and leads us into a process of restoration. He literally takes all the junk we have inflicted on ourselves and turns it into a trophy of restoration. When we turn to Him in our failures, He weaves a tapestry of divine beauty in us.

In the previous chapters I described the many times that I chose the wrong road. But thank God, He brought me back to Himself, back to the narrow path that leads to healing. I repented of my deadly choices. I confessed all of the times I chose paths that were not motivated by love. Nevertheless, I will often be tempted to leave God's path. I love how *The Message* paraphrases the apostle Paul's lament regarding his struggle with sin:

> The moment I decide to do good, sin is there to trip me up. I truly delight in God's commands, but it's pretty obvious that not all of me joins in that delight. Parts of me covertly rebel, and just when I least expect it, they take charge. I've tried everything and nothing helps. I'm at the end of my rope. Is there no one who can do anything for me? Isn't that the real question? The answer, thank God, is that Jesus Christ can and does. He acted to set things right in this life of contradictions where I want to serve God with all my heart and mind, but am pulled by the influence of sin to do something totally different. (Rom. 7:21–25)

The path to healing and new life is so narrow that we must follow the footsteps of Jesus as He clears the way for us through the forest of sin and certain death. Then and only then, somewhere along the path we will unexpectedly experience moments of true healing and abundant life.

THE BIRTH OF HOPE

A word of caution: restoration is often a slow process. Sometimes it takes a lifetime. Perhaps it will never fully happen until we reach heaven. We must give the enormous power of sin its due; it never disappears with the wave of a magic wand. But the God of grace gives us second chances. In fact I would like to tell how one of my self-inflicted wounds has been slowly and painfully healed.

The promiscuity of my early adult life—what I considered to be "free love"—ended up costing me dearly. Because sexual sin involves intense intimacy between two humans, it almost always has enduring consequences. There were times along the way when I thought that, through faith, I had achieved some measure of healing. But then the consequences would come back to haunt me, often in camouflaged forms. Like a virus that "disappears" and then reemerges to cause more painful symptoms, my sexual sin has been a source of deep and often unexpected trouble.

Too often the powerful and continued consequences of sexual sin are downplayed. I never cease to be amazed by the pervasiveness of those consequences. Once, after speaking to more than two thousand students at Baylor University, I was rudely brought to a new awareness of my depravity. My motivation for speaking was a good one: I wanted to help the young people avoid making the same mistakes I had made as a student there some twenty years before. I hoped to warn them about the consequences of sexual sin. I was the one, however, who was taught a powerful lesson.

After I was introduced by the chaplain, who had warned me not to let the students' inattention shake me, I began my speech. I would have loved to stand before them as some big shot or "alumnus made good," but I was compelled to honestly reveal who I was and what I had been through.

"I came to this school twenty years ago as a student to get a Christian education," I began, "but instead, I got a girl pregnant."

I listened to the rush of wind as all of the newspapers were folded and notebooks closed. I obviously had gotten their attention. Even though it was not easy, I told them the truth: I paid for half of the abortion costs; that, after all, was the least I could do to get rid of what I had considered a mere "inconvenience"; I never stopped to think about what I was doing; the realization that I had murdered my child almost cost me my life. Because of the guilt and inner turmoil, I'd had ulcers eating at my stomach, intestines, and colon.

What I experienced has been labeled male postabortion syndrome, which is marked by the powerful guilt and shame that result when a person commits an act of genocide. The despair, emptiness, and pain are overwhelming. The guilt is often increased by the fact that the man, who is supposed to protect the mother and child after conception, has instead become a destroyer of life. I explained to the students that although male postabortion syndrome is less traumatic than what the woman usually experiences, it is nonetheless real.

I also told them how I had struggled spiritually for two years before I could accept the forgiveness that was available to me through Christ. My life got worse before it got better. My physician told me that in order to live, I would need surgery or something miraculous would have to change in my life. Accepting Christ's forgiveness was the only miracle I needed. As I began to heal spiritually, my physical condition improved as well. Over time, the internal scars disappeared, and tests by my physicians in the years ahead would reveal no trace of the trauma.

As I gave my speech, I realized that if my child had been given the opportunity to live, she would have been about the age of these students and could have been in the audience. That thought grieved me. The speech had been tremendously draining, but I felt it was worth it. Several students lined up to talk with me afterward, many of whom struggled with secret sexual sins.

Shortly after giving my talk at Baylor, I received a phone call. It was from the girl I had gotten pregnant all those years ago. We talked for a while, and she told me God had also restored her, though not without much pain and struggle. Then she confronted me.

"The next time you tell the story," she said, "be more honest about what really happened."

I was confused. I thought I had been as honest as possible. "What do you mean?" I asked.

She reminded me that I didn't just help pay for the abortion; I had *pressured* her to get it. She had never wanted to do it. She wanted to give birth to the baby and raise it or put it up for adoption. My forcefulness and manipulation led her to abort the child against her will. Once again, through the truth, the consequences of my sin painfully resurfaced.

The phone call forced me to see who I really am. Because

of my cowardice, I had persuaded a wonderful person to assist me in ending a life. Facing the truth about myself wasn't a pleasant experience, but I needed to do it to complete the healing process.

A Cycle of Healing

The pattern of healing became a familiar one to me: truth, despair, repentance, healing. Each time I realized the truth about my sins and their consequences, the cycle repeated itself. I wish I could say that my problems ended with a single instance of repentance; they did not. Sometimes I would avoid the truth or slip away from my faith and revert to old patterns. Rather than face the truth about myself, I was always tempted to return to the broad and easy path of destruction. Relief seemed easier than healing; comfort was preferable to honesty.

The narrow path to grace seems inexpressibly difficult because acts of repentance and faith are painful. I gradually made my way back to a whole and healthy relationship with God, but not before I obtained counseling and worked through many issues with the help of an accountability group. Through these measures, I learned to live out my commitment to a God-honoring lifestyle.

At that time, after so much progress in my life, I came to realize there would be no kids due to the continued infertility. I was struck anew with sorrow, depression, and a sense of personal failure. The irony never escaped me. Once, when I could create life, I had ended it. Now I could not create it even though I desperately wanted to.

Our emotional pain was compounded when some Christians suggested that our infertility was God's judgment. They concluded that my past sexual sin was keeping us from having children. Those insensitive and misguided remarks almost undid what I had finally resolved with God—that He does forgive and offer second chances. I have always found it amazing how other Christians can hold a grudge at the same time God offers grace.

THE SURPRISES OF LIFE

At times the process through which God took us seemed unbearably difficult, almost cruel. Once, after I spoke at a crisis pregnancy center fund-raiser, a pregnant woman approached my wife and me and asked if we would want her baby. Although we hadn't talked much about adoption, we were instantly excited and pursued the process with a counselor. As it turned out, the counselor was upset with the woman because she had not consulted her, and she manipulated the woman into withdrawing the offer. Like thousands of others who are rejected in the adoption process, we were devastated. It seemed as if God had placed a carrot in front of us, then removed it at the last second. It was simply too much to bear, and after that incident, we no longer considered adoption to be a viable option for us. We could not deal with that kind of rejection and pain again.

For another year we remained mired in our quiet desperation. We had resigned ourselves to remaining childless. Then
in July 1990, I was asked to speak to a group of four thousand
black charismatic Christians in Atlanta, Georgia, which was
unusual because I am neither black nor charismatic.

After I spoke, a woman approached me and said, "God has
given me a message for you."

For a second I squirmed: I had just bought a new car, and
I thought maybe God was going to tell me to give it back. But
that wasn't the case.

She continued, "The Lord told me that you are going to
receive a gift—a baby."

I nodded politely and said, "Thank you for your concern,
but I'm afraid we can't have children. We've gone through years
of testing, and we're infertile."

That same day, July 3, 1990, I met my friend and pub-
lisher Victor Oliver for lunch. Unexpectedly he inquired
about our plans for children. I brought him up to date on our
long struggle.

"Well," Victor said, "here's something to think about. My
best friend's sixteen-year-old daughter is pregnant. She and her
boyfriend have decided not to abort the child, and they're
looking for a Christian couple to raise their baby. Would you
be interested?"

The next day, Independence Day, we met with the couple.
We fell in love with them and marveled at their courage. They
wanted their baby to have all the things that they, being young

and unestablished, knew they couldn't provide. This couple obviously loved their unborn child.

After much deliberation they decided to give us their baby. They phoned us with the news, and we began preparing the house and taking baby classes. Late Christmas Eve, we were awakened by a phone call with the news that the baby had been born. The next day, Christmas, we flew to Atlanta to meet our little girl. We spent the next couple of days with the baby's father as they made their final evaluations. When our baby was finally handed over, the nurse placed her in my arms. What a moment! Never before or since in my life have I so powerfully understood God's amazing grace.

This young couple lovingly gave up their child so she could have the best possible life and an infertile couple could have the best possible lives. These courageous people represent all who allow couples like us to become parents.

I, who for so long had struggled with my sin and our infertility, was handed this gift of new life. What a gracious and creative God! He had restored what I had so carelessly destroyed years ago. We knew that this kind of joy could come only from God.

The narrow path to restoration was difficult, but God's surprising grace was always there. He wanted what was best for me, so He allowed me to face the truth about myself, bringing me to real repentance. And in His perfect timing, He surprised me with His incredible grace—and the gift of life.

THE AUTHENTIC CHURCH

As I have traveled around, I have had the great opportunity to speak in some wonderful churches. I attend one now. Sadly, this has not always been the case. Many of us were raised to believe that we must not embarrass the church or ourselves by revealing our sins. We are, instead, allowed to fudge a little on the truth, if it makes the church look better and its people more perfect. I was taught that the church was where hurting people came to hide, lest anyone think they may be lacking in their faith. I thought God was a faker, since that was what I was used to in church.

It was a great surprise, then, to find that God's true vision of the church is for hurting, vulnerable, sinning, and sick people to come together to heal in the midst of the Holy Spirit. God never hid the realities of His family. The disciples, after walking with Christ Himself, doubted Him, lied about knowing Him, betrayed Him, and got into some of the most egotistical conversations ever recorded. The physical presence of Jesus did not produce perfection in the hearts of His disciples. Why should we expect perfection from ourselves?

God works with those who are authentic in their faith. They don't fake it because they have no need to. What they look like to God means more than what they look like to people. Revealing their own struggles and encouraging others to reveal theirs is more important than protecting themselves

from the attacks of vicious gossips who lurk about in the hall-
ways of every spiritually dead church.

God wants a real church with real people who are brave
enough to face the truth about themselves and humble enough
to share it with others. When that happens, the life of the
church begins. Dead churches are playing hide-and-seek.
Vibrant churches are safe places for people to be nothing more
or less than who they really are. No revival ever ripped through
a church, town, or country without at least one brave soul who
decided to stop faking it and start coming out into the open
about his condition. If you want to lead the charge for Christ,
lead out into the open. Lay your heart bare for others to examine and you will be surprised what God can do with you and
those who follow your lead.

CONCLUSION

The surprise of infinite grace is a life-changing surprise. It is the
motivation that keeps me going and trying to tell as many
people about it as I can. It is my only hope—otherwise, I would
face a life of certain condemnation because I know I am not
good enough to earn my way to heaven. Except for God's grace,
I just don't have what it takes. If you do not know this about
God, if you are leading a life under condemnation, I invite you
to the banquet table of our Lord who wants to fellowship with
sinners like you and me. Please take a Bible and do a study on
God's grace until you are certain you can feel it in your soul. You

will be surprised at what God will do through you when you start responding to His grace rather than your failures.

That's it. I have finished this book about the second chances God has given me. I am so grateful that you read the book and trusted me to introduce you to some of those chances. If God has given you second chances that mean a lot to you, I would love to hear from you. You can reach me by writing to: Stephen Arterburn, P.O. Box 1018, Laguna Beach, CA 92652, or just e-mail me at SArterburn@newlife.com

A final note: One of the greatest joys of my life over the past few years has been to meet the people who run crisis pregnancy, adoption agencies, and those who fight for the lives of the unborn. Please support these organizations and centers with your prayers, your volunteer time, and your money. They need our support to turn tragedies into triumphs, to turn a crisis into an opportunity for God's healing grace and surprising power of restoration.

NOTES

CHAPTER TWO

1. See Steve Arterburn and Jack Felton, *Toxic Faith* (Nashville: Thomas Nelson, 1991).
2. Ibid.
3. For further information about the "prosperity gospel" and other misguided forms of religion, see *Toxic Faith*.

ABOUT THE AUTHOR

Stephen Arterburn is the founder and chairman of New Life Ministries, the nation's largest faith-based broadcast, counseling, and treatment ministry and is also the host of the nationally syndicated *New Life Live!* daily radio and television program, heard on more than two hundred stations across America and around the world on Sirius XM Radio and the Internet.

Arterburn is the creator of the Woman of Faith® conferences, attended by more than seven million women, and a best-selling author with more than seven million books in print, including *Every Man's Battle*, *Healing Is a Choice*, and *Regret-Free Living.*

He has appeared on numerous nationally televised talk shows and has been featured in publications such as *The New York Times*, *USA Today*, and *The Wall Street Journal.* He resides with his family in Fishers, Indiana. He is married to a wonderful and brilliant woman of faith, and they live with their kids, Madeline (19 and away at college), Carter (12), James (10), and the latest additions, Solomon (3) and Amelia Pearl (9 months). *Yes, there is great joy there!*

To contact Steve, e-mail him at SArterburn@newlife.com.

Transforming Lives
Through God's Truth

New Life Ministries is a non profit organization, founded by author and speaker, Stephen Arterburn. Our mission is to identify and compassionately respond to the needs of those seeking healing and restoration through God's truth.

New Life's ministry of healing and transformation includes:

- *A daily call-in radio program, New Life Live!*
- *A nationwide counseling network*
- *Life changing weekend workshops*
  New Life Weekend
  Every Man's Battle
- *Group Coaching*
- *Treatment for Drug and Alcohol addiction*
- *Books, CDs, Podcasts and others resources*
- *National Call Center*

**For more information
call 1-800-NEW-LIFE (639-5433) or
visit newlife.com**

The
NEW LIFE
Weekend

So often we pray for God to take our challenges and life issues away, and we wait and wait for Him to act; when in reality He's waiting for us to do what we're asking Him to do. New Life weekend is your opportunity to take that first step towards healing and the beginning of a transformed life.

weekend

"This weekend, I was able to break through layers of hurt, easily what would have taken a year in therapy."
-Terrie

This weekend includes main sessions taught by Steve Arterburn with small-group counseling sessions led by a Christian counselor focusing on:

- Anger
- Balancing Your Life
- Body Image/Weight Loss
- Creating Boundaries
- Depression

- Fear/Anxiety
- Forgiveness
- Getting Unstuck
- Grief
- Marriage (Enhance, Rescue or Restore)

- Post-abortive Healing
- Restoring a Wife's Heart
- Self Worth and Confidence
- Surviving Sexual Abuse

"It was like a warm hug from the Lord-it's a hug that never lets go."
- Jill

"Thank the Lord for how he uses your ministry and has saved my marriage." - Janet

1-800-NEW-LIFE   newlife.com

Lust...Porn...Affairs... They've taken your spiritual life to a place you never imagined. It's a serious problem that requires a serious solution. The Every Man's Battle Workshop is the place where men engage in the battle to get back their sexual integrity. In this intensive three-day workshop you'll work with licensed Christian counselors who will arm you with the weapons you need for victory. **The enemy may have wounded you, but the battle is not over.**

with host
Steve Arterburn

and co-hosts

Dr. Henry Cloud | Dr. John Townsend | Dr. Dave Stoop | Milan Yerkovich | Dr. Jill Hubbard

Listen to *New Life Live!* radio on stations across the
country. To find a station near you call
1-800-NEW-LIFE or
go to www.newlife.com
You can also listen online.
To be on the show, call 1-800-229-3000.

"See you on the radio..."

Are you hurting?
Are you looking for counseling or
are in need of some answers?

Call our New Life Call Center
at **1-800-NEW-LIFE** (639-5433)

1-800-NEW-LIFE   newlife.com